D0573459

Other atlases in the PLUTO PROJECTS series:

THE NEW STATE OF THE WORLD ATLAS
by Michael Kidron and Ronald Segal
4th edition 1991

THE STATE OF THE EARTH ATLAS
by Joni Seager
2nd edition (forthcoming) 1994

THE NEW STATE OF WAR AND PEACE
by Michael Kidron and Dan Smith
2nd edition 1991

THE STATE OF HEALTH ATLAS
by Judith Mackay
1st edition 1993

THE STATE OF THE UNITED STATES
by Doug Henwood
1st edition (forthcoming) 1994

THE STATE OF RELIGION ATLAS

THE STATE OF RELIGION ATLAS

Joanne O'Brien and Martin Palmer
Consultant Editor: David B. Barrett

A PLUTO PROJECT

A TOUCHSTONE BOOK
Published by Simon & Schuster
New York London Toronto Sydney Tokyo Singapore

TOUCHSTONE
Simon & Schuster Building
Rockefeller Center
1230 Avenue of the Americas
New York, New York 10021

Text copyright © 1993 Joanne O'Brien and Martin Palmer
Maps copyright © 1993 Myriad Editions Limited, London

All rights reserved
including the right of reproduction
in whole or in part in any form

Published in Great Britain by
Simon & Schuster Ltd., London

Edited and coordinated for Myriad Editions by Anne Benewick
with Candida Lacey

Maps created by Swanston Graphics Limited, Derby, England
Artwork and design by Isabelle Lewis
with Andrew Bright and Jeanne Radford

Additional design by Corinne Pearlman

Printed and bound in Hong Kong
Produced by Mandarin Offset Ltd.

10 9 8 7 6 5 4 3 2 1 ppb

Library of Congress Cataloging-in-Publication Data
available on request

ISBN 0-671-79376-4

CONTENTS

INTRODUCTION 11

PART 1:

PRESENT AND PAST

1 POPULAR RELIGIONS 16
Majority religions by state

2 ARRIVALS 18
Arrivals, since 1450, of today's majority religions

3 ROOTS AND BRANCHES 20
Majority religions by main denomination, school or sect

BELIEFS

4 CHRISTIANITY AND ISLAM 22
Worldwide strength of the two largest religions

5 HINDUISM 24
Hindus as a proportion of state populations

6 BUDDHISM 26
The revival of Buddhism in Asia and beyond

7 THE JEWISH DIASPORA 28
Jews as a proportion of state populations

8 THE SIKHS 30
Sikh populations and gurdwaras

9 TRADITIONAL BELIEFS 32
Survival of local, tribal beliefs

10 NEW RELIGIOUS MOVEMENTS 34
Their origins and centres

11 UNITED DIVERSITY 36
The growth of Protestant denominations in the USA

12 FAITH IN THE FEMININE 38
Female deities and religious figures

13 DOUBTS AND CERTAINTIES 40
Agnostics, atheists and humanists

PART 2:

REACHING OUT

14 THE MISSION 44
The Christian missionary movement

15 A WORLDWIDE CHURCH 46
The Roman Catholic network

16 ON AIR 48
Christian and other religious broadcasting

17 CHRISTIAN GIVING 50
Christian aid agencies

18 MUSLIM GIVING 52
Muslim aid agencies

19 INTEREST IN MONEY 54
Islamic banking

THE STATE

20 STATE FAIR – AND UNFAIR 56
Religious freedom and state control

21 LIFE AND SOUL OF THE PARTY 58
Political party links to the majority religions

22 GENERATION TO GENERATION 60
Religious education

23 GOD AND MAMMON 62
State financial support for majority religions

24 ISLAMIC LAW 64
The legal system and courts in Islamic states

25 RELIGIONS AT WAR 66
The role of religion in wars and civil wars

CHALLENGES

26 NEVER AGAIN? 68
The effects of the Holocaust and anti-semitism in the 1990s

27 FAITH TO FAITH 74
The inter-faith movement

28 THE ECUMENICAL MOVEMENT 70
Christian unity and division

29 EQUAL RITES 72
The status of women within the majority religions
30 DOWN TO EARTH 76
Environmental campaigns and the religions
31 FAITH IN THE FUTURE 78
Estimated strength of the majority religions by 2025

PART 3:
THE HEARTLANDS
32 FOUNDATIONS 82
Places associated with the origin and development of the major religions
33 HOLY CITIES 84
Cities and towns as centres of religion
34 HOLY NATURAL 86
Islands, mountains and rivers as pilgrimage centres

FUNDAMENTALS OF THE FAITHS
Buddhism, Christianity, Hinduism, Islam, Judaism, Sikhism, Taoism

THE NATURE OF GOD 88
THE CREATION 89
TIME 90
LIFE AFTER DEATH 91
SACRED LITERATURE 92
PROPHETS AND FOUNDERS 93
RITES OF BIRTH AND DEATH 94
FESTIVALS 95

NOTES AND SOURCES 96

INTRODUCTION

Medieval theologians are reputed to have tried to work out how many angels could dance on the head of a pin. A data-based assessment of the worldwide state of religion today has at times felt like a similar task!

This atlas shows at a glance the major contours of the religious world, as summed up within the formal structures of the major faiths and the relationships between them. The maps also highlight effectively the position of the major faiths in relation to important contemporary issues such as the environment and the status of women. In working on this unique project, we have all been conscious of both its strengths and weaknesses. Given the sheer diversity of worldwide religious belief we have found it necessary to give more emphasis to the major faiths than is perhaps justified. There are hints of this wider diversity in map 9. Traditional Beliefs, and map 10. New Religious Movements, but inevitably, with maps conceived on a global scale and in limited space, the local and unquantifiable has often had to be lost.

This atlas deals primarily, therefore, with the worlds of Buddhism, Christianity, Hinduism, Islam, Judaism, Sikhism and traditional beliefs as a group, including Chinese popular religion. In deciding on what issues to cover in the maps, we were obviously constrained by those which could be illustrated and on which we could offer substantial and reliable evidence. However, not all religious organizations consider the production of regular, statistical annual reports as being an essential part of their faith! To find appropriate subjects with sufficient data, we have sifted through materials from around the world, benefitting in the process from the unrivalled database of David B. Barrett.

Many of these maps represent the fullest and most up-to-date information available, as in the maps on popular religions (map 1) and on the Christian missionary movement (map 14). In other maps, on Christian and Muslim giving, for example (maps 17 and 18), we have merely tried to give a feel for a vast area and identified particular aid agencies to show the spread of such work worldwide. In some maps we have tried to focus on wider phenomena, as in the map on holy cities (map 33). And yet others illustrate ideas that are currently much-debated and even highly controversial, such as female deities (map 12), Islamic banking (map 19) and the future of the major faiths (map 31).

The pictures which emerge of the state of religion are quite stark. The maps give substance to issues and developments in ways which may be unexpected: on the continued rise of Christianity and Islam and the consequential demise of traditional religions; on the re-emergence of religion, following the collapse of Communism, and the consequent tendency to diversification; on the extent of formal ties between individual religions and states; and on the scale of religious involvement in warfare.

This is the first attempt to convey worldwide religious diversity in maps of this kind. While we have sought to find and use all relevant data, there are surely many sources which have remained untapped by us. The next edition, we hope, will not only be more up-to-date, but will tackle topics for which, this time round, available data was simply inadequate. The wealth of the major faiths is but one example of a topic we would like to have covered, but we could neither find relevant data nor agree on appropriate criteria. If you have information which may contribute to, refute, or expand a topic dealt with here, do please let us know, citing your source.

As authors, we have relied heavily upon friends and colleagues from the different faiths, all of whom are acknowledged, either on the maps themselves or in the notes to the maps at the back of the atlas. The most invaluable aid has been offered by our consultant editor, David B. Barrett, a mine of information, without whose pioneer work we could never have considered undertaking this task. Our thanks also to all our colleagues in the International Consultancy on Religion, Education and Culture (ICOREC). Finally, our thanks to our editor, Anne Benewick, whose vision this atlas originally was and whose tireless work has helped us on our way.

Joanne O'Brien
Martin Palmer
Manchester, June 1993

Part 1

PRESENT AND PAST BELIEFS

Copyright © Myriad Editions Limited

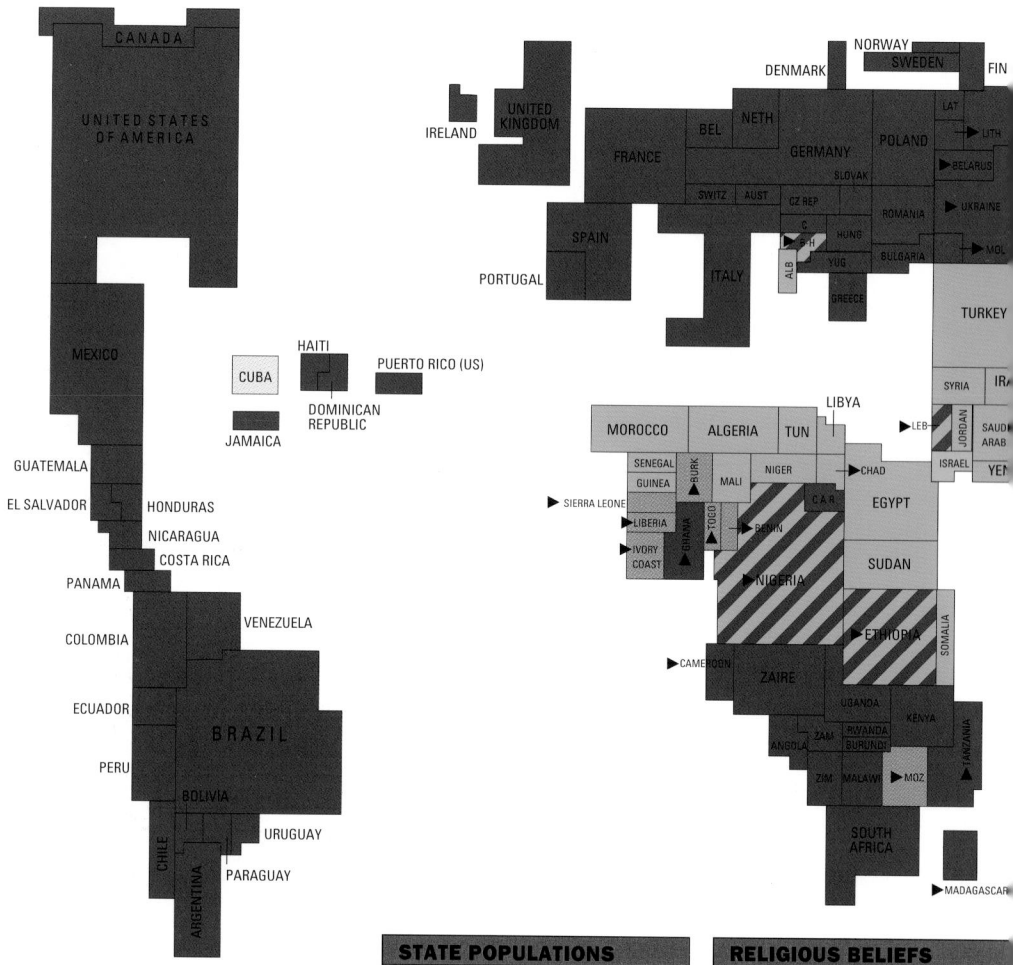

STATE POPULATIONS

STATES' SHARES OF WORLD POPULATION *mid-1990* percentages

= 1%

= below 0.1% of world population

RELIGIOUS BELIEFS

MOST POPULAR RELIGION OF EACH STATE
allegiance claimed by at least 66 percent of population

- Buddhism
- Christianity
- Hinduism
- Islam
- Judaism
- Chinese indigenous religion
- other indigenous beliefs
- official atheism
- ▶ religion of majority but less than 66% claim allegiance

Sources: Population Reference Bureau; D.B. Barrett, *World Christian Encyclopedia*, 1982; I. Harris and others, *Contemporary Religions*, 199 F. Shaikh, ed. *Islam and Islamic Groups*, 1992; P. Harvey, *Introduction to Buddhism*, 1990; press reports

26 states: together less than 0.3% of world population

BAHAMAS BARBADOS BELIZE BERMUDA ▶BOTSWANA CAPE VERDE CYPRUS (S) CONGO EQUATORIAL GUINEA ▶ ESTONIA GABON GRENADA GUYANA ICELAND LESOTHO LUXEMBOURG MALTA NAMIBIA SAO TOME SEYCHELLES SLOVENIA SOLOMON ISLANDS ▶ SURINAME SWAZILAND TONGA ▶ TRINIDAD & TOBAGO

13 states: together less than 0.2% of world population

BAHRAIN ▶ BRUNEI COMOROS CYPRUS (N) DJIBOUTI GAMBIA KUWAIT MALDIVES MAURITANIA OMAN QATAR UNITED ARAB EMIRATES WESTERN SAHARA

▶ GUINEA-BISSAU
▶ MAURITIUS
▶ FIJI

less than 0.05% of world population

BHUTAN ▶ MONGOLIA

POPULAR RELIGIONS 1

In more than 80 percent of the world's states at least two thirds of the population claim allegiance to a single faith. For Christians in Europe this is no indication of regular church attendance.

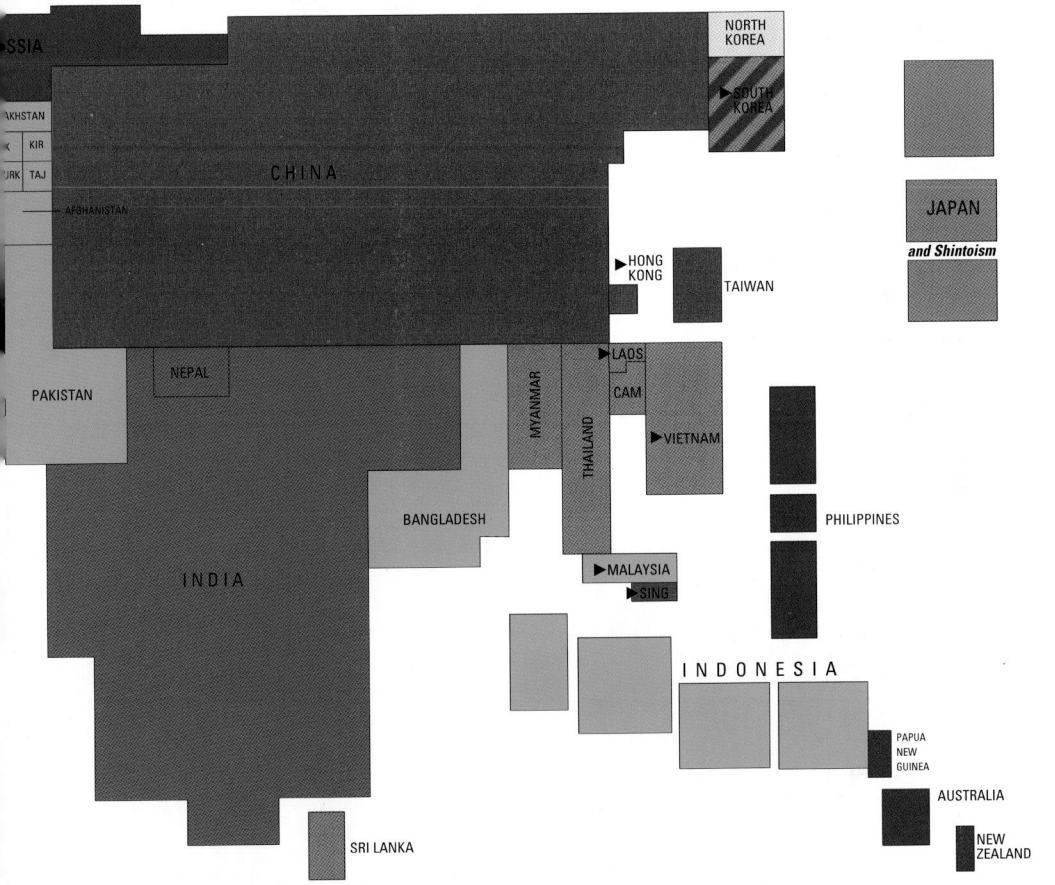

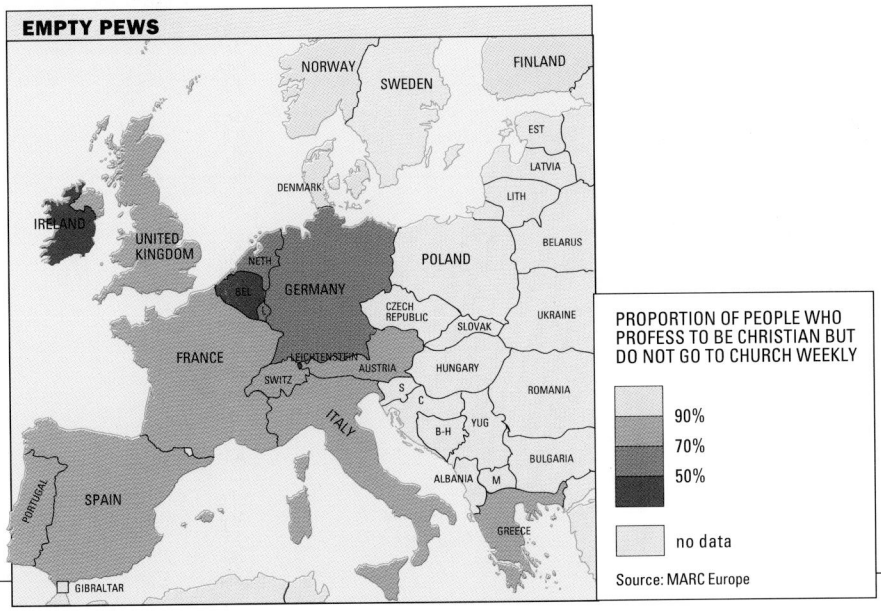

Copyright © Myriad Editions Limited

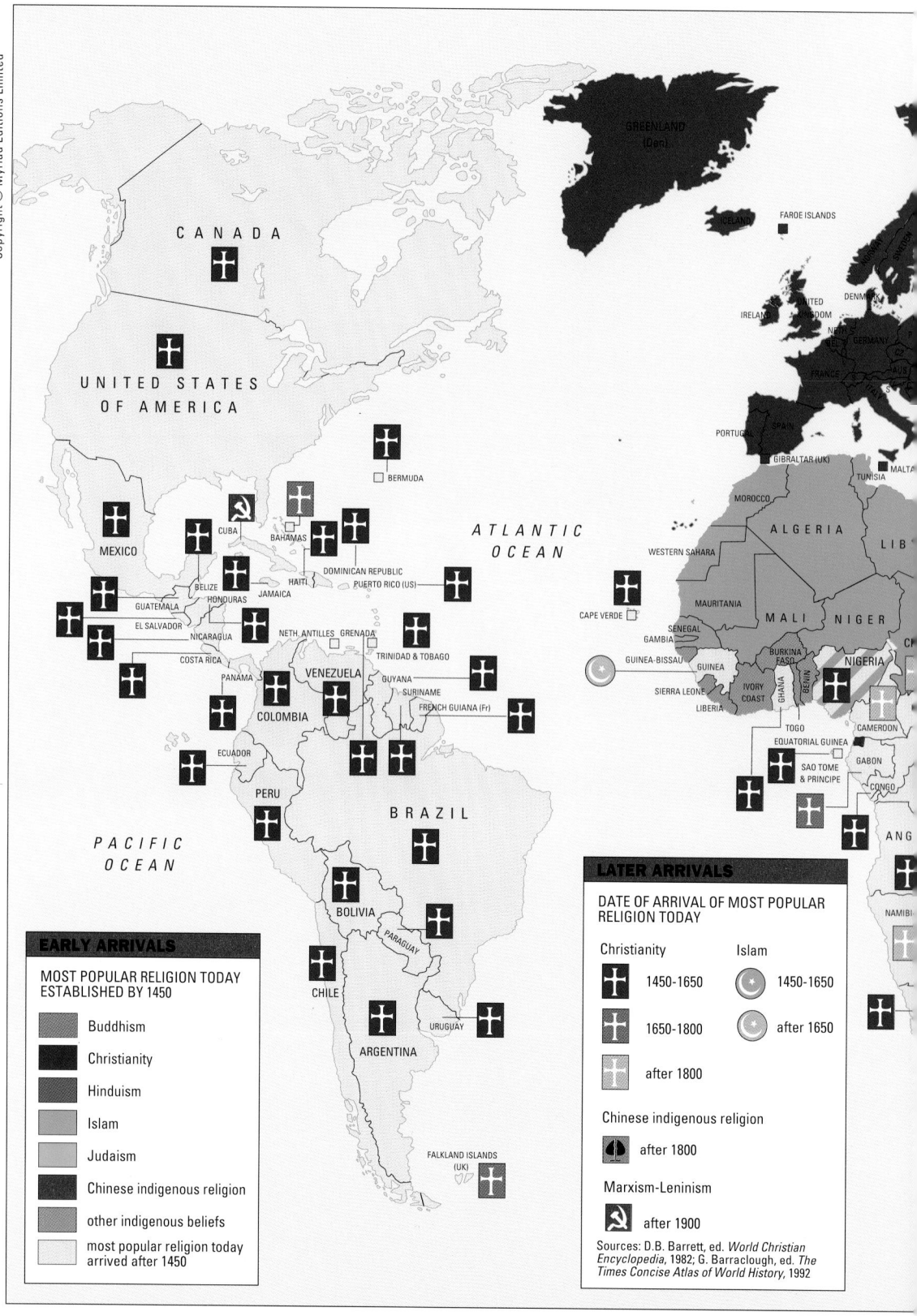

Over the last 500 years, Christianity has gained more new followers than any other religion, usually replacing local indigenous religions.

Copyright © Myriad Editions Limited

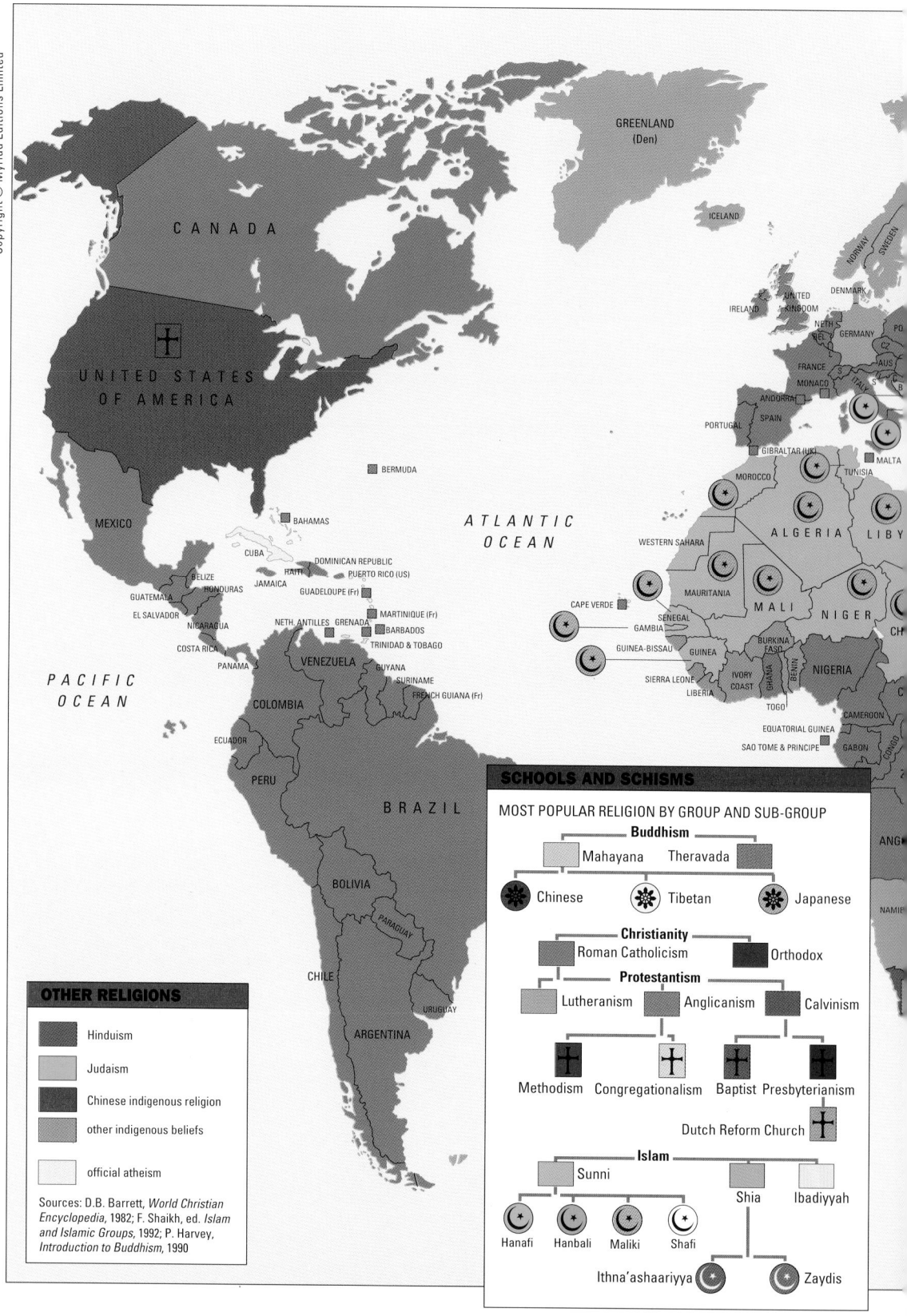

ROOTS AND BRANCHES 3

Yesterday's revolution can be today's orthodoxy. Some new movements have grown to become the most popular religion in a state.

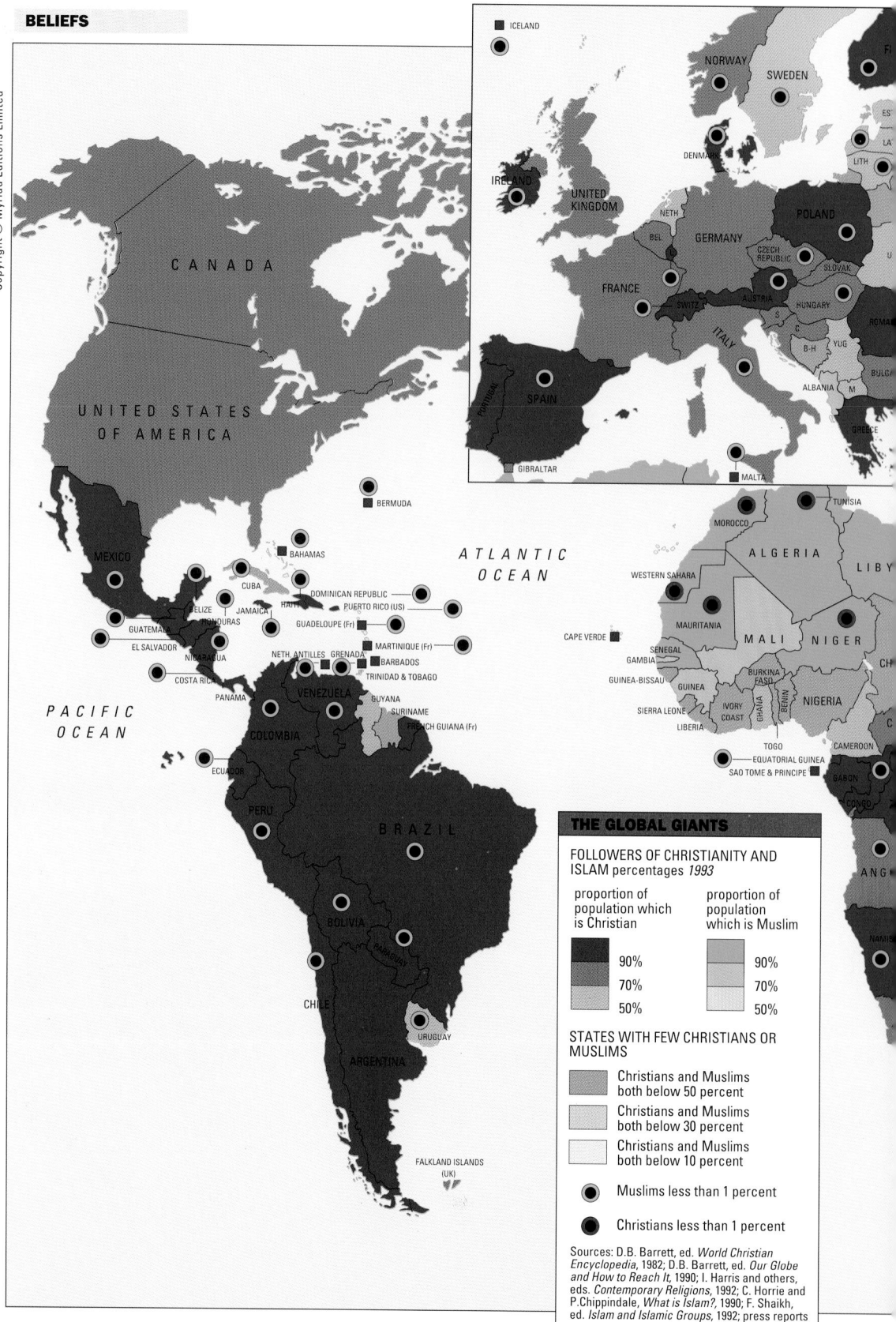

Copyright © Myriad Editions Limited

CHRISTIANITY AND ISLAM 4

Nearly half the world claims allegiance to the two largest faiths: over a billion to Islam, nearly two billion to Christianity.

Copyright © Myriad Editions Limited

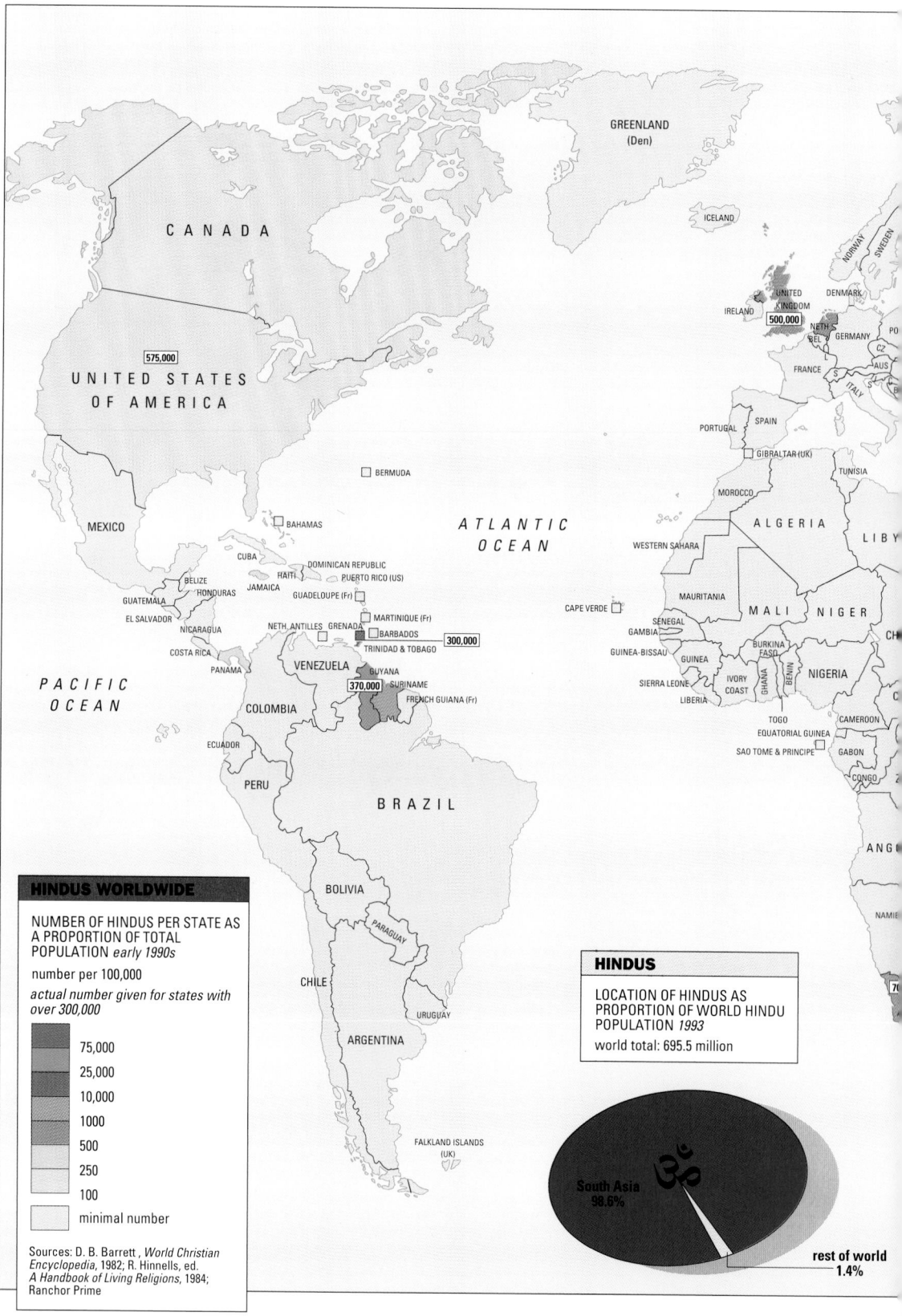

There are nearly 750 million Hindus worldwide. Almost all live in South Asia. Many of the overseas communities have grown in areas linked to the trading routes of colonial powers.

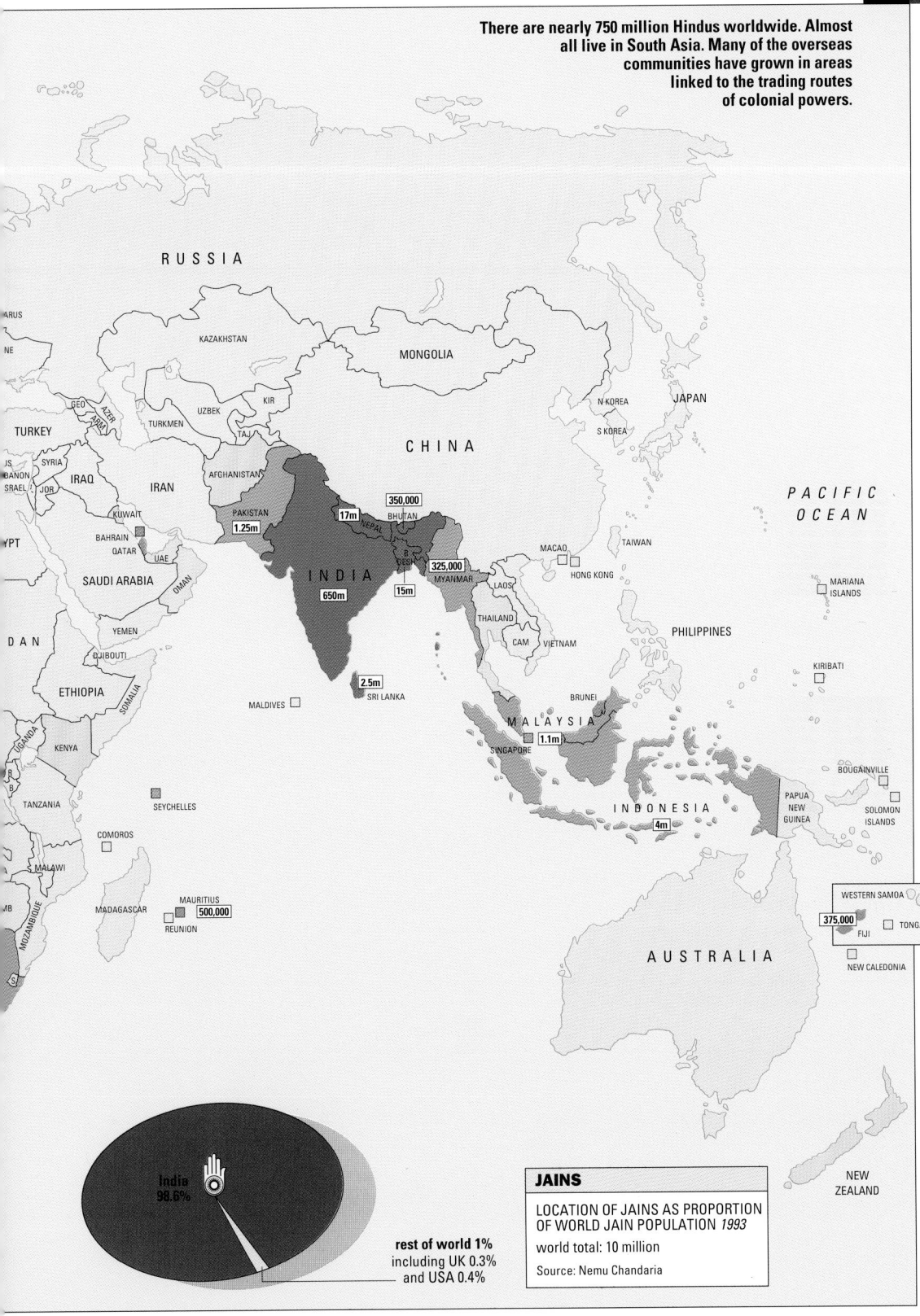

JAINS

LOCATION OF JAINS AS PROPORTION OF WORLD JAIN POPULATION *1993*

world total: 10 million

Source: Nemu Chandaria

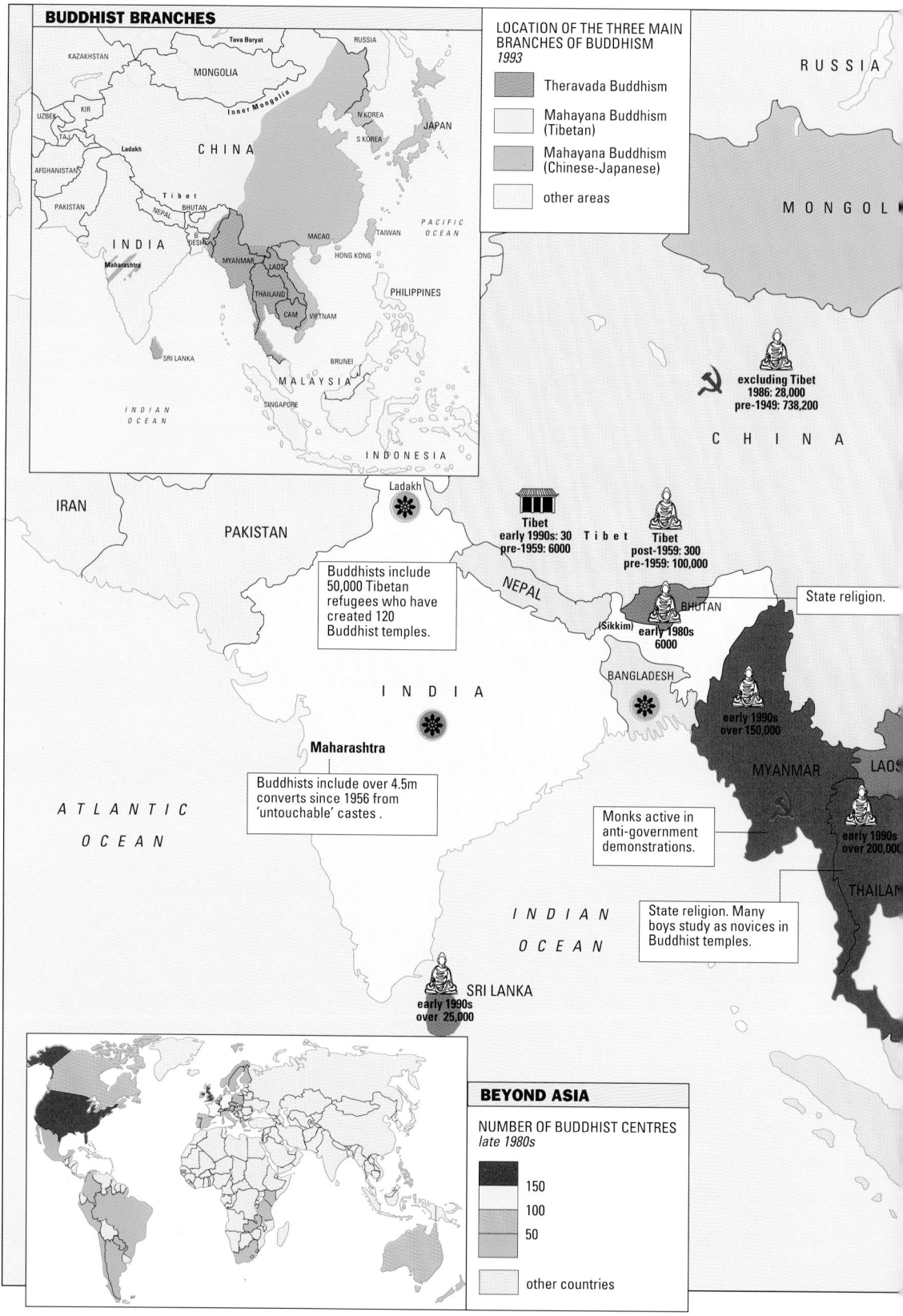

Copyright © Myriad Editions Limited

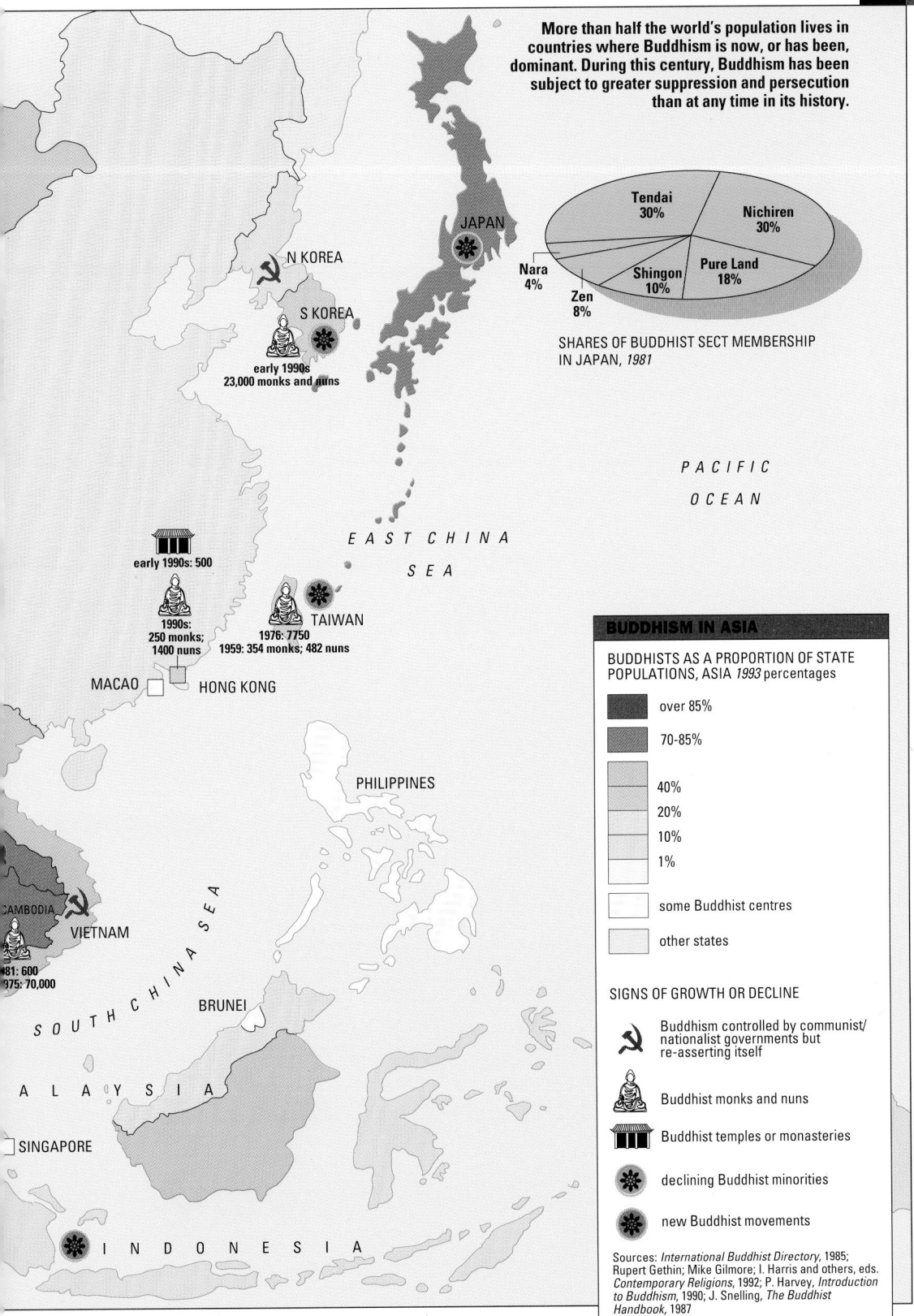
More than half the world's population lives in countries where Buddhism is now, or has been, dominant. During this century, Buddhism has been subject to greater suppression and persecution than at any time in its history.
Tendai 30%
Nichiren 30%
Pure Land 18%
Shingon 10%
Zen 8%
Nara 4%
SHARES OF BUDDHIST SECT MEMBERSHIP IN JAPAN, *1981*
JAPAN
N KOREA
S KOREA
early 1990s 23,000 monks and nuns
PACIFIC OCEAN
EAST CHINA SEA
early 1990s: 500
1990s: 250 monks; 1400 nuns
TAIWAN
1976: 7750
1959: 354 monks; 482 nuns
MACAO
HONG KONG
PHILIPPINES
CAMBODIA
VIETNAM
981: 600
975: 70,000
SOUTH CHINA SEA
BRUNEI
A L A Y S I A
SINGAPORE
I N D O N E S I A
BUDDHISM IN ASIA
BUDDHISTS AS A PROPORTION OF STATE POPULATIONS, ASIA *1993* percentages
over 85%
70-85%
40%
20%
10%
1%
some Buddhist centres
other states
SIGNS OF GROWTH OR DECLINE
Buddhism controlled by communist/ nationalist governments but re-asserting itself
Buddhist monks and nuns
Buddhist temples or monasteries
declining Buddhist minorities
new Buddhist movements
Sources: *International Buddhist Directory*, 1985; Rupert Gethin; Mike Gilmore; I. Harris and others, eds. *Contemporary Religions*, 1992; P. Harvey, *Introduction to Buddhism*, 1990; J. Snelling, *The Buddhist Handbook*, 1987

Copyright © Myriad Editions Limited

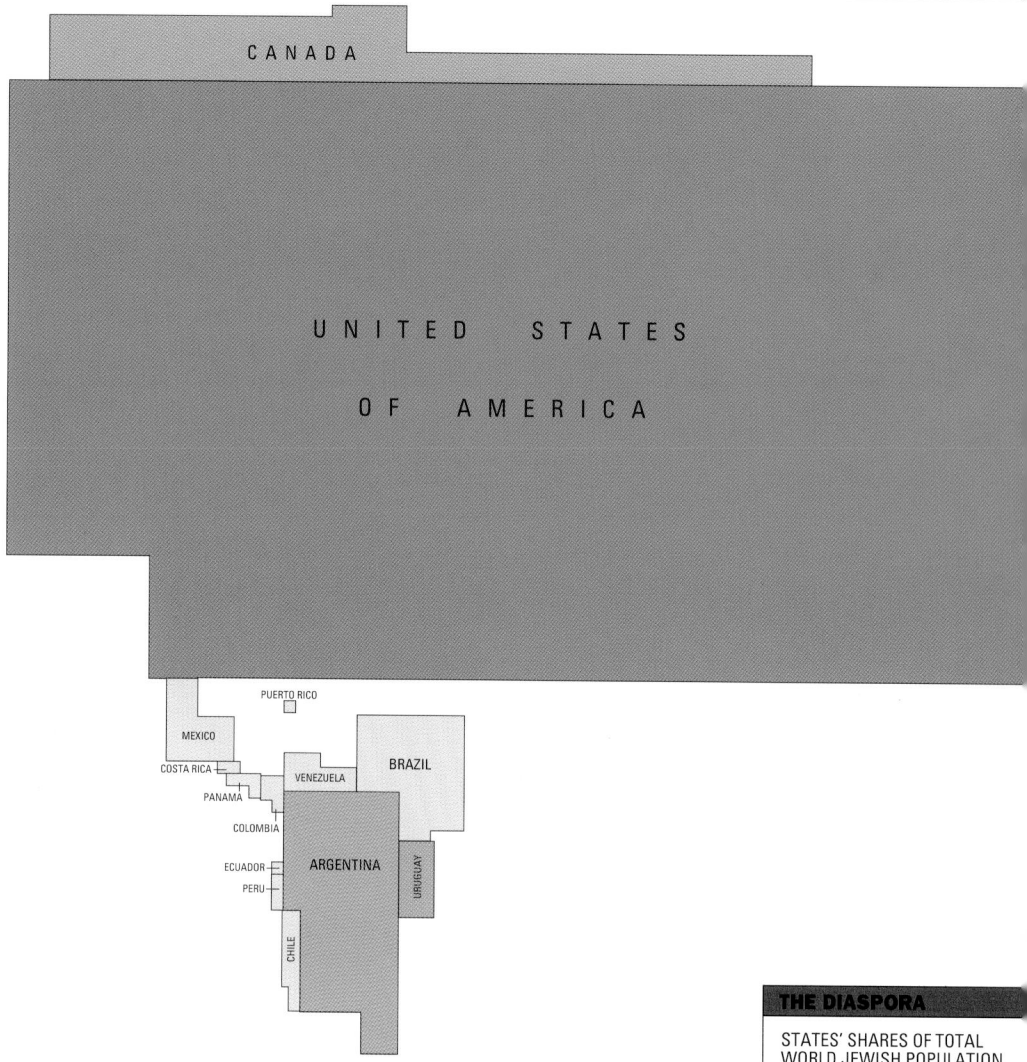

JEWS IN 1800

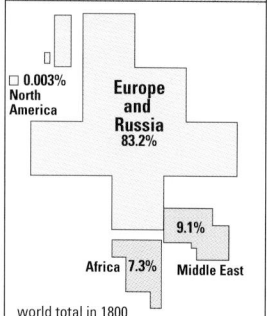

world total in 1800
3·28 million

JEWS IN 1993

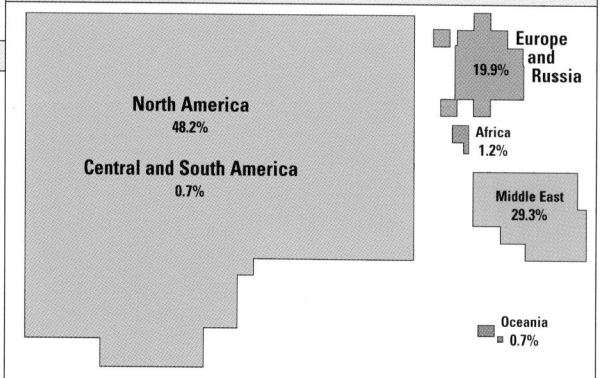

world total in 1993
12.8 million

SHARES OF WORLD JEWISH POPULATION BY REGION *1800 and 1993* percentages

=10%
=1%
=0.1%

THE DIASPORA

STATES' SHARES OF TOTAL WORLD JEWISH POPULATION *1990*

Size of state indicates its percent share of world total: 12.8 million

= 1% (128,000)
= 0.1% (12,800)
= 0.01% (1280)

NUMBER OF JEWS IN EACH STA PER 1000 POPULATION *1990*

819
22
7
5
3

Sources: D. Singer, ed. *The American Jewish Yearbook*, 1992; Board of Deput of British Jews

There are 12.8 million Jews worldwide who identify themselves as Jewish, though not all are religious Jews. Over 96 percent live in just 12 states.

SWEDEN
FINLAND
ESTONIA
LATVIA
LITHUANIA
BELARUS
UKRAINE
RUSSIA
ELAND
UNITED KINGDOM
DENMARK
NETHS
POLAND
GERMANY
BELGIUM
SWITZ.
FORM. CZECH.
AUSTRIA
MOLDOVA
KAZAKHSTAN
AZER
GEORGIA
UZBEKISTAN
TURKMENISTAN
KIRGHIZIA
TAJIKISTAN
TURKEY
IRAN
INDIA
SYRIA
HUNGARY
ROMANIA
BULGARIA
GREECE
FRANCE
ITALY
SPAIN
ISRAEL
YEMEN
MOROCCO
TUNISIA
ETHIOPIA
SOUTH AFRICA
OTHER STATES
AUSTRALIA
NEW ZEALAND

THE OLIM

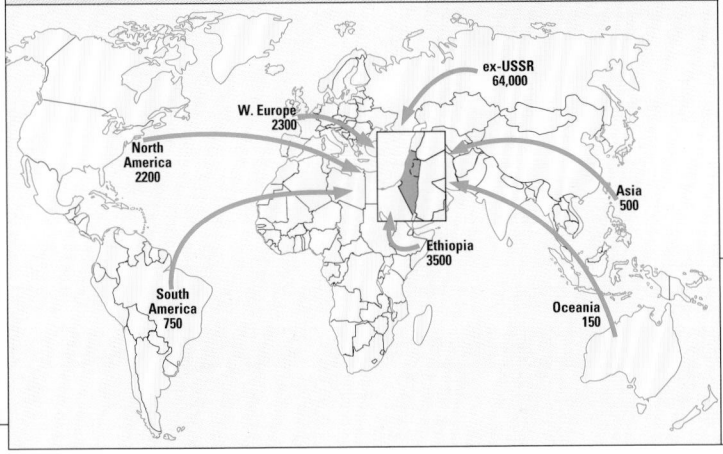

IMMIGRANTS ARRIVING IN ISRAEL
January-December 1992

Total 76,000

numbers and origin

Source: Jewish Agency, Jerusalem

Copyright © Myriad Editions Limited

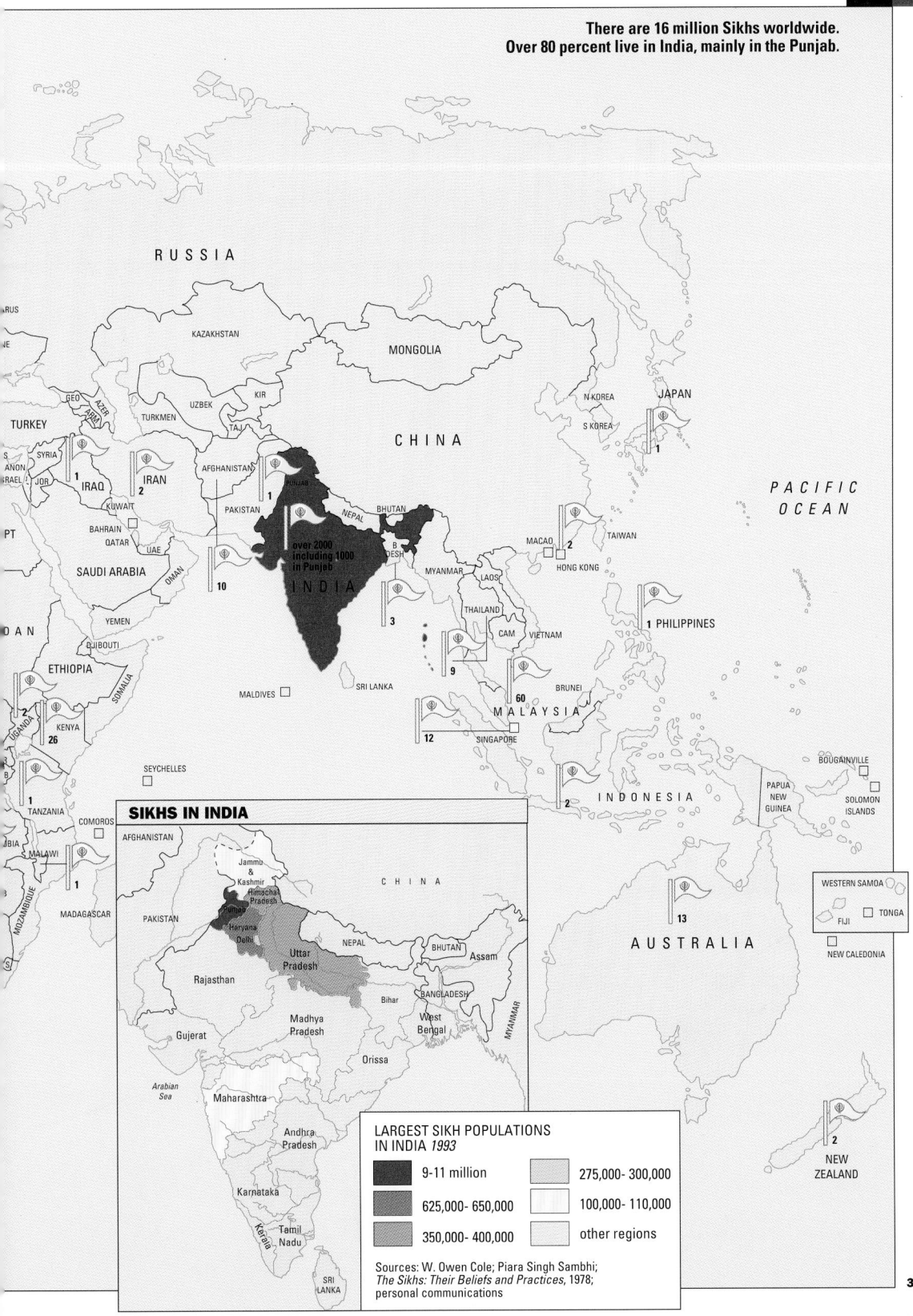
There are 16 million Sikhs worldwide.
Over 80 percent live in India, mainly in the Punjab.
RUSSIA
KAZAKHSTAN
MONGOLIA
CHINA
JAPAN
N KOREA
S KOREA
TURKEY
SYRIA
IRAQ
IRAN
KUWAIT
BAHRAIN
QATAR
UAE
SAUDI ARABIA
OMAN
YEMEN
DJIBOUTI
ETHIOPIA
SOMALIA
KENYA
UGANDA
TANZANIA
COMOROS
MALAWI
MADAGASCAR
MOZAMBIQUE
SEYCHELLES
MALDIVES
SRI LANKA
AFGHANISTAN
PAKISTAN
NEPAL
BHUTAN
B DESH
MYANMAR
LAOS
THAILAND
CAM
VIETNAM
MACAO
HONG KONG
TAIWAN
PHILIPPINES
BRUNEI
MALAYSIA
SINGAPORE
INDONESIA
PAPUA NEW GUINEA
BOUGAINVILLE
SOLOMON ISLANDS
WESTERN SAMOA
FIJI
TONGA
NEW CALEDONIA
AUSTRALIA
NEW ZEALAND
PACIFIC OCEAN
over 2000 including 1000 in Punjab
INDIA
SIKHS IN INDIA
Jammu & Kashmir
Himachal Pradesh
Punjab
Haryana
Delhi
Uttar Pradesh
Rajasthan
Gujerat
Madhya Pradesh
Bihar
Assam
West Bengal
Orissa
Maharashtra
Andhra Pradesh
Karnataka
Tamil Nadu
Kerala
Arabian Sea
LARGEST SIKH POPULATIONS IN INDIA 1993
9-11 million
625,000- 650,000
350,000- 400,000
275,000- 300,000
100,000- 110,000
other regions
Sources: W. Owen Cole; Piara Singh Sambhi; The Sikhs: Their Beliefs and Practices, 1978; personal communications

Copyright © Myriad Editions Limited

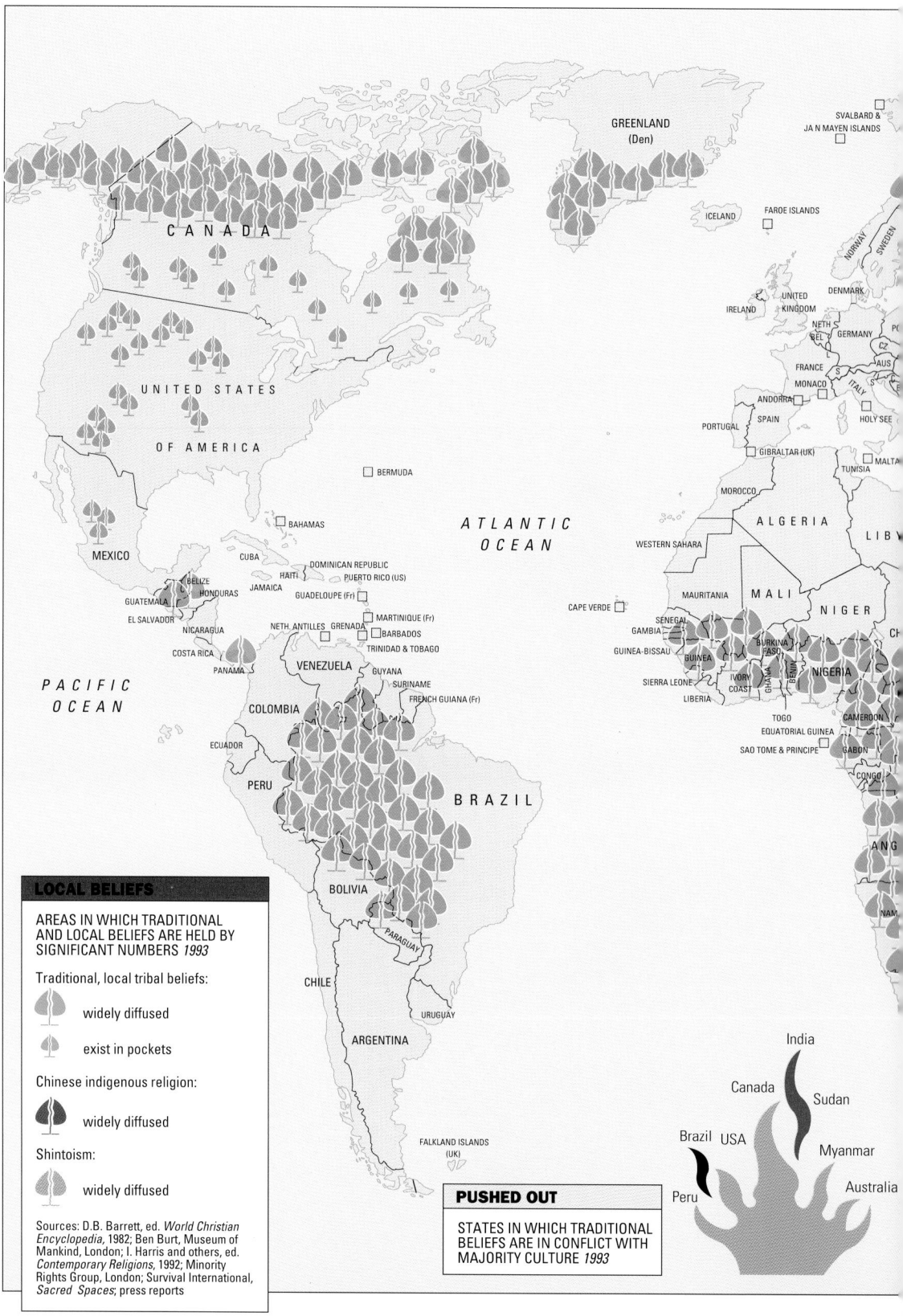

LOCAL BELIEFS

AREAS IN WHICH TRADITIONAL AND LOCAL BELIEFS ARE HELD BY SIGNIFICANT NUMBERS *1993*

Traditional, local tribal beliefs:

widely diffused

exist in pockets

Chinese indigenous religion:

widely diffused

Shintoism:

widely diffused

Sources: D.B. Barrett, ed. *World Christian Encyclopedia*, 1982; Ben Burt, Museum of Mankind, London; I. Harris and others, ed. *Contemporary Religions*, 1992; Minority Rights Group, London; Survival International, *Sacred Spaces*; press reports

PUSHED OUT

STATES IN WHICH TRADITIONAL BELIEFS ARE IN CONFLICT WITH MAJORITY CULTURE *1993*

TRADITIONAL BELIEFS 9

Traditional and local beliefs vary widely. They are closely related to the land and have often survived where it is difficult or inaccessible. Many people belong to a major world religion while continuing to hold traditional local beliefs.

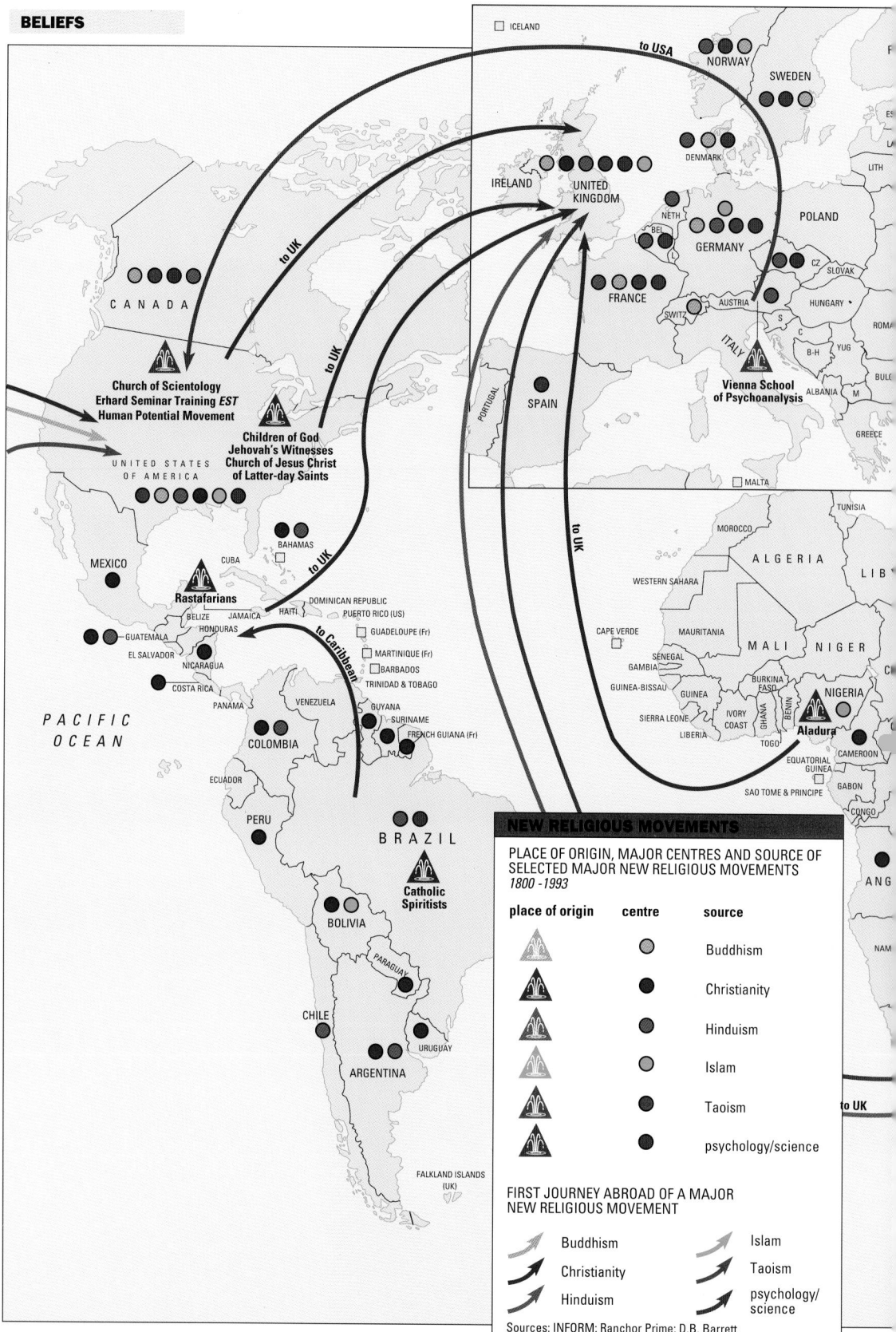

Copyright © Myriad Editions Limited

NEW RELIGIOUS MOVEMENTS 10

The migration of people and ideas fosters 'new religious movements'. Most but not all have their origin in a major world religion. A small minority achieve a high profile as a result of unconventional and even criminal activities.

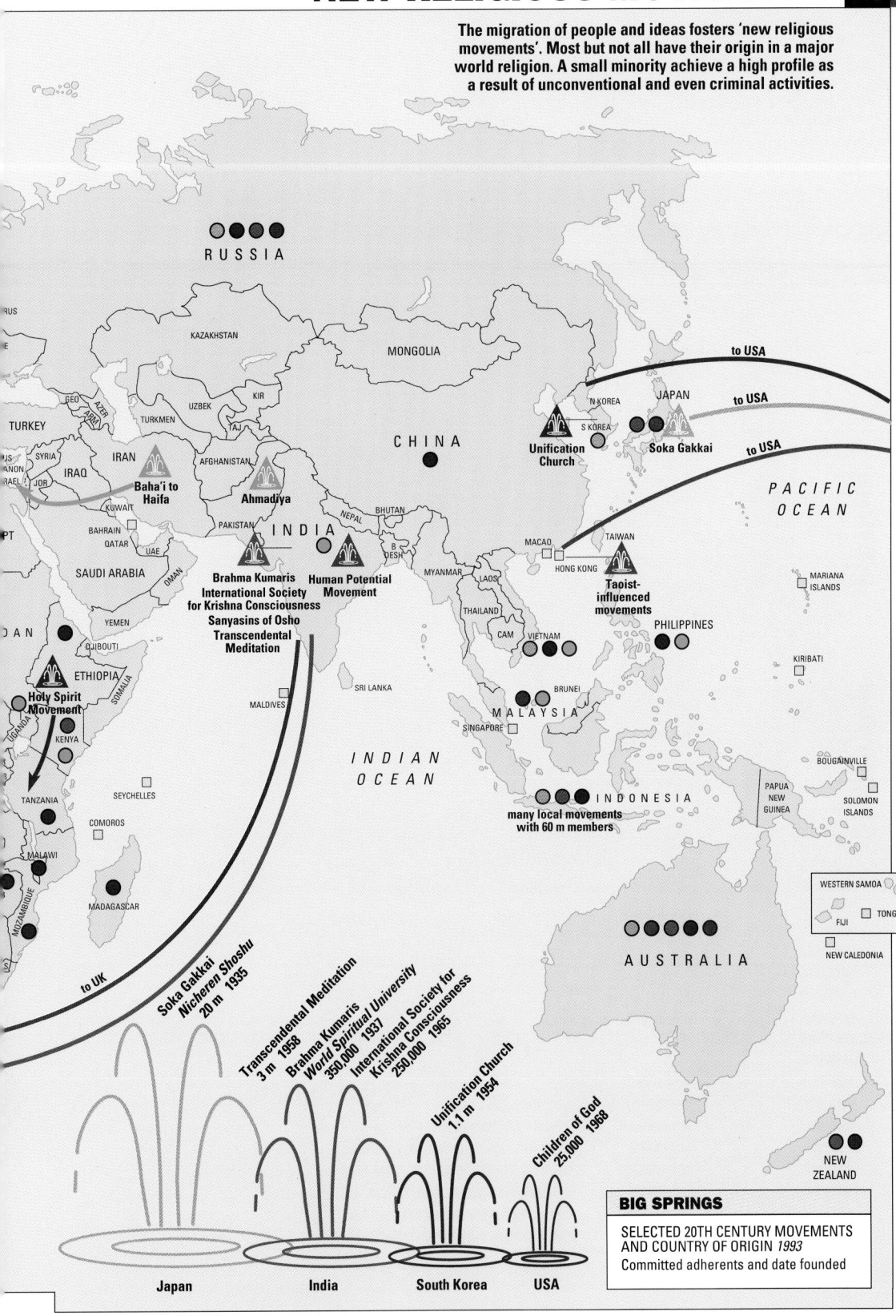

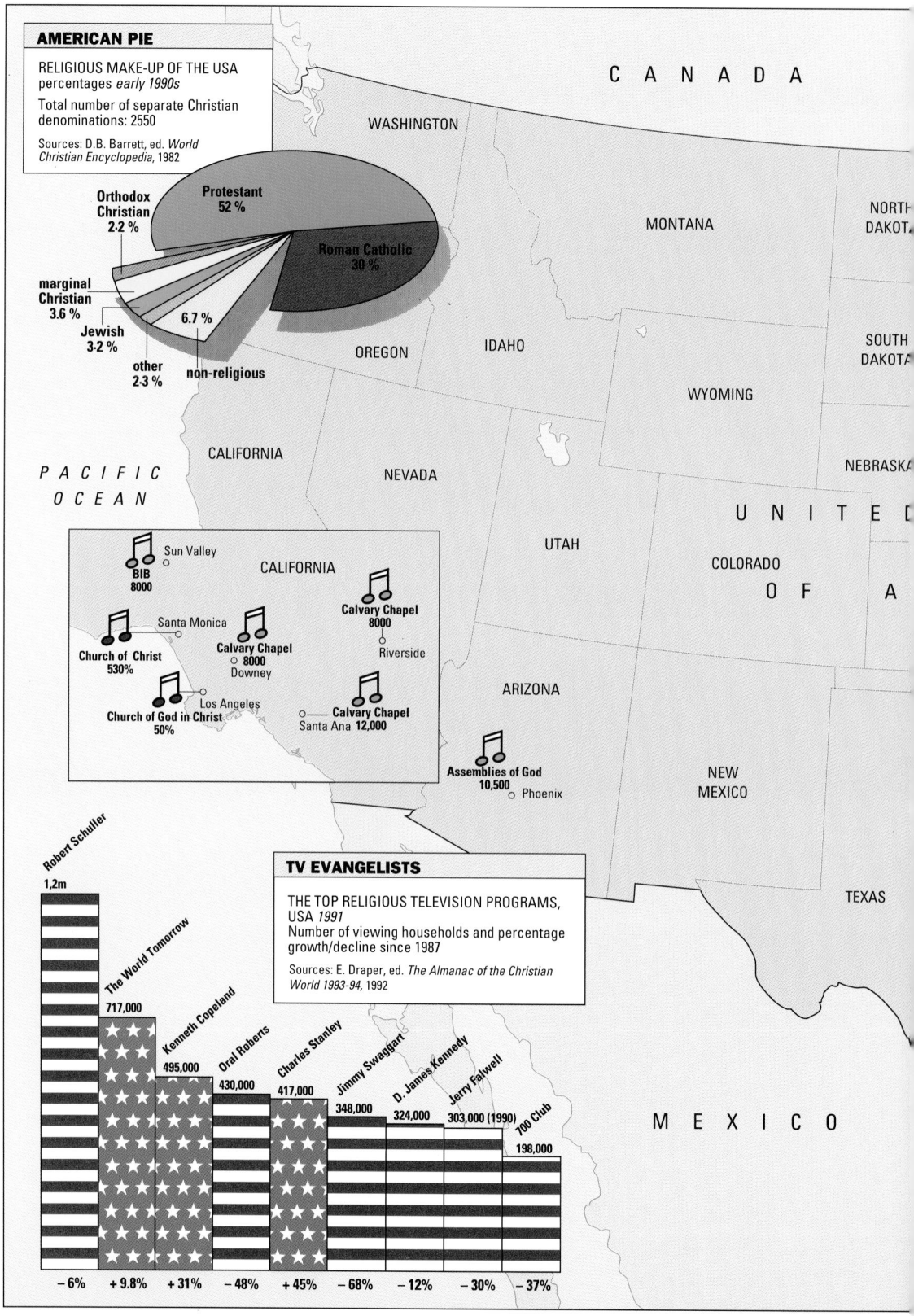

Copyright © Myriad Editions Limited

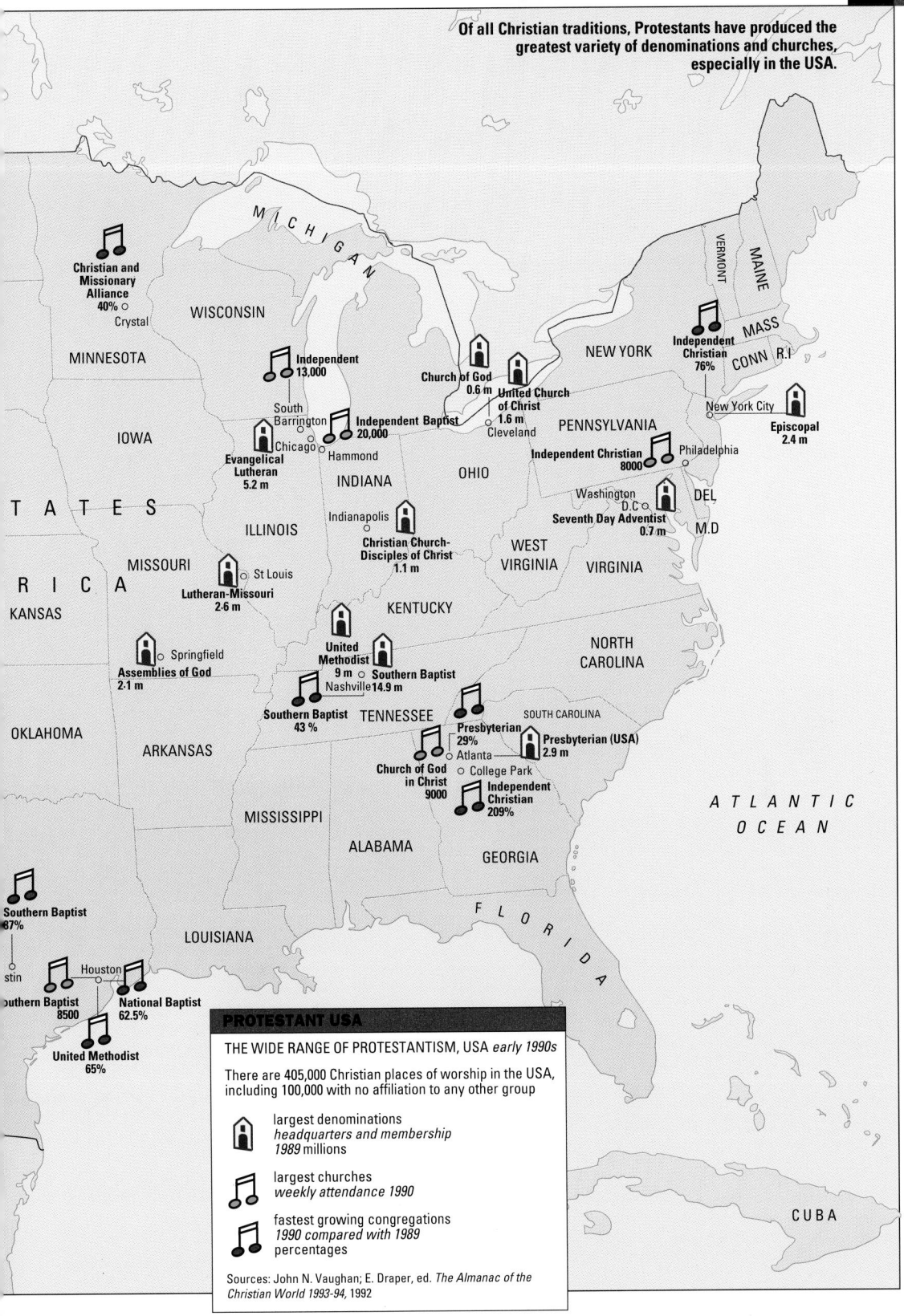
Of all Christian traditions, Protestants have produced the greatest variety of denominations and churches, especially in the USA.
MICHIGAN
Christian and Missionary Alliance 40%
Crystal
WISCONSIN
MINNESOTA
Independent 13,000
South Barrington
Chicago
Hammond
Independent Baptist 20,000
Evangelical Lutheran 5.2 m
IOWA
Church of God 0.6 m
United Church of Christ 1.6 m
Cleveland
NEW YORK
VERMONT
MAINE
Independent Christian 76%
MASS
CONN
R.I
New York City
Episcopal 2.4 m
PENNSYLVANIA
Independent Christian 8000
Philadelphia
INDIANA
OHIO
Washington D.C
Seventh Day Adventist 0.7 m
DEL
M.D
Indianapolis
Christian Church-Disciples of Christ 1.1 m
ILLINOIS
WEST VIRGINIA
VIRGINIA
MISSOURI
St Louis
Lutheran-Missouri 2·6 m
KANSAS
KENTUCKY
Springfield
Assemblies of God 2·1 m
United Methodist 9 m
Southern Baptist 14.9 m
Nashville
NORTH CAROLINA
Southern Baptist 43 %
TENNESSEE
SOUTH CAROLINA
Presbyterian 29%
Presbyterian (USA) 2.9 m
Atlanta
Church of God in Christ 9000
College Park
Independent Christian 209%
OKLAHOMA
ARKANSAS
MISSISSIPPI
ALABAMA
GEORGIA
ATLANTIC OCEAN
Southern Baptist 87%
stin
Houston
Southern Baptist 8500
National Baptist 62.5%
United Methodist 65%
LOUISIANA
FLORIDA
CUBA
PROTESTANT USA
THE WIDE RANGE OF PROTESTANTISM, USA early 1990s
There are 405,000 Christian places of worship in the USA, including 100,000 with no affiliation to any other group
largest denominations
headquarters and membership
1989 millions
largest churches
weekly attendance 1990
fastest growing congregations
1990 compared with 1989
percentages
Sources: John N. Vaughan; E. Draper, ed. The Almanac of the Christian World 1993-94, 1992

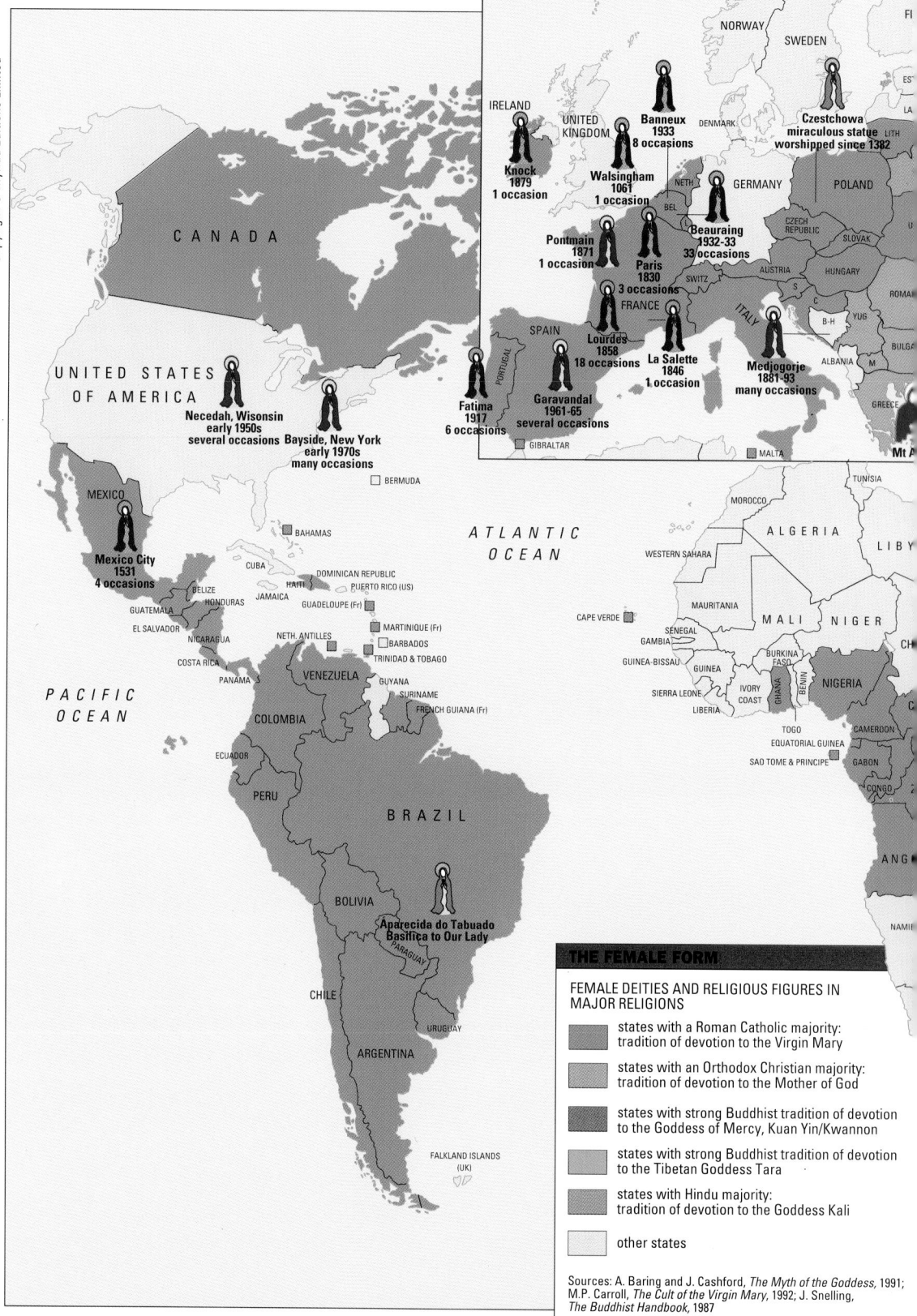

Copyright © Myriad Editions Limited

FAITH IN THE FEMININE 12

All major religions are patriarchal, though some contain within them strong devotional traditions associated with female deities or religious figures.

Copyright © Myriad Editions Limited

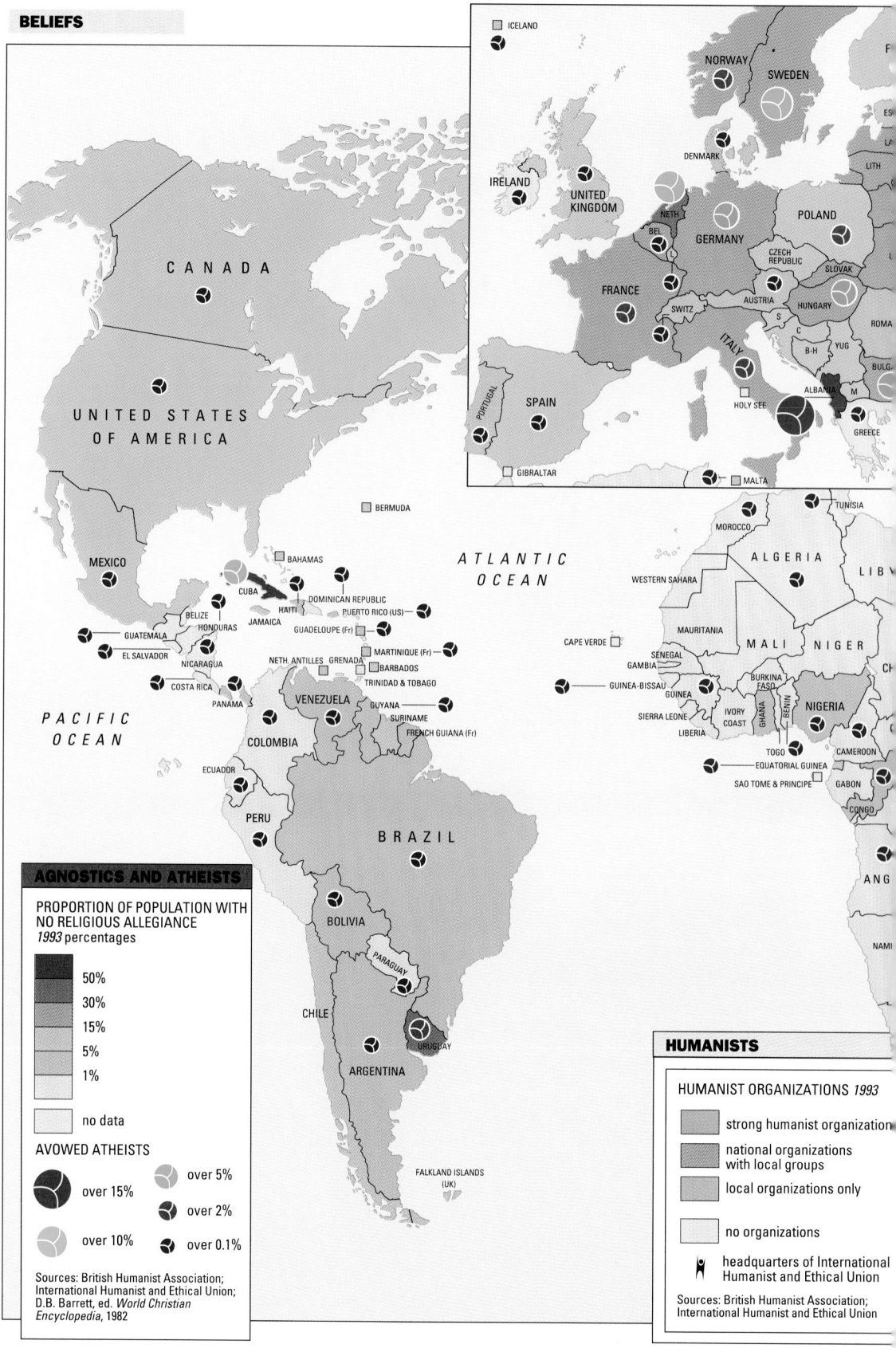

DOUBTS AND CERTAINTIES 13

Over 20 percent of the world's population does not claim any allegiance to a religion. Most are agnostics. Others are atheists, who deny the existence of God.

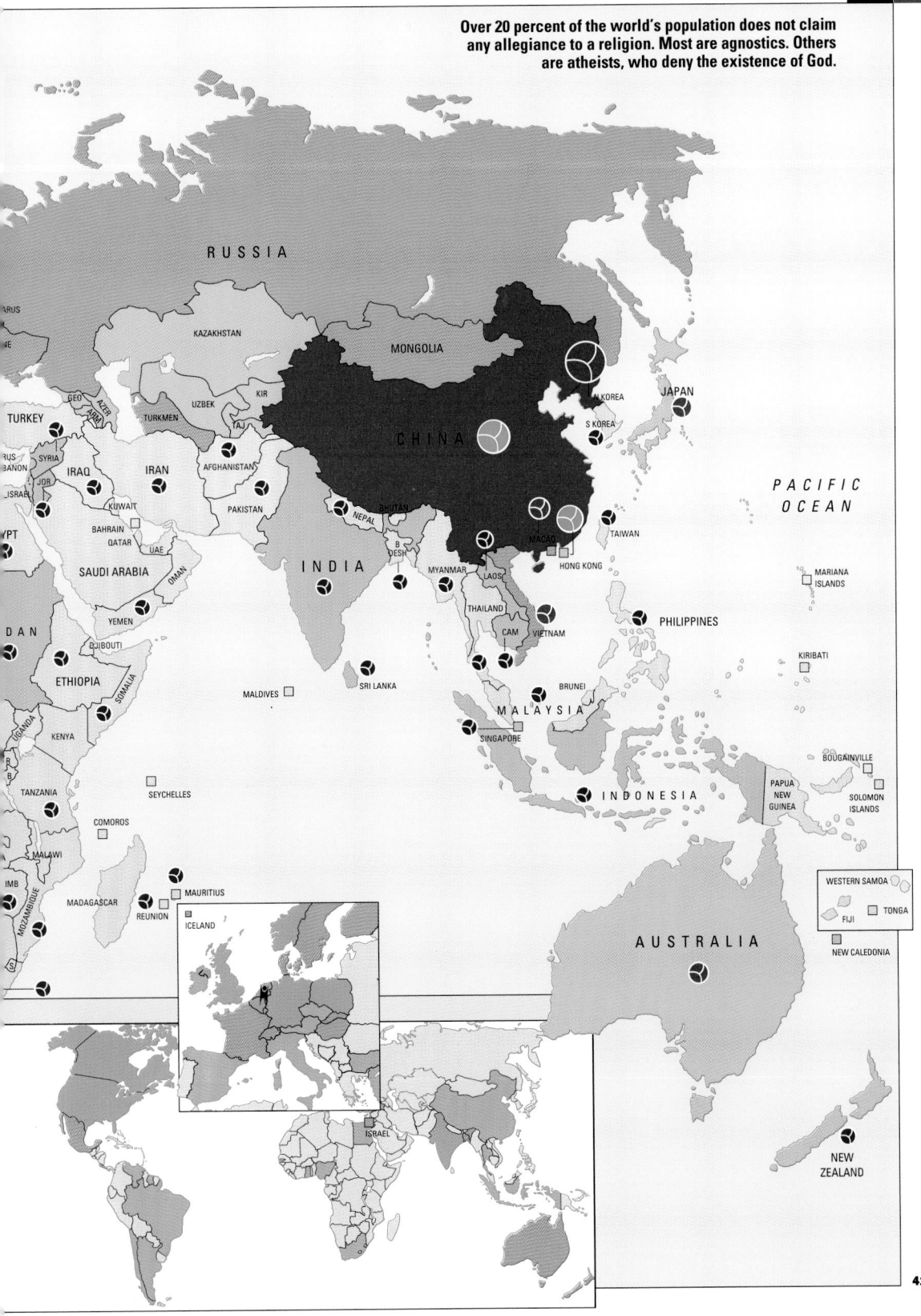

Part 2

REACHING OUT
CHALLENGES

Copyright © Myriad Editions Limited

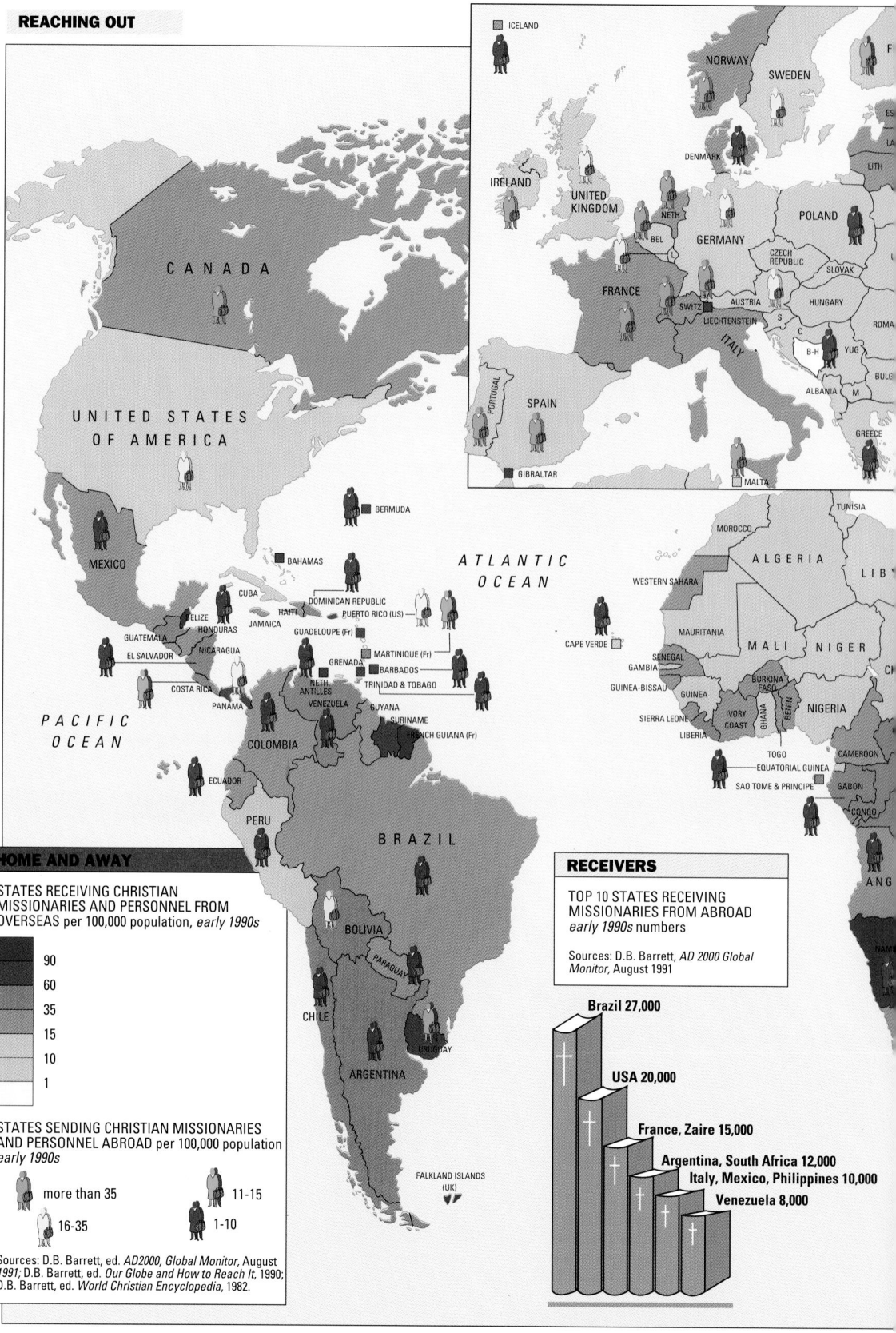

There are more than 300,000 Christian missionaries worldwide. Some are evangelists only, but many work on social, health and education projects.

Copyright © Myriad Editions Limited

A WORLDWIDE CHURCH 15

The Pope heads a global network which stretches out to 900 million Roman Catholics, one-sixth of the world's population.

Copyright © Myriad Editions Limited

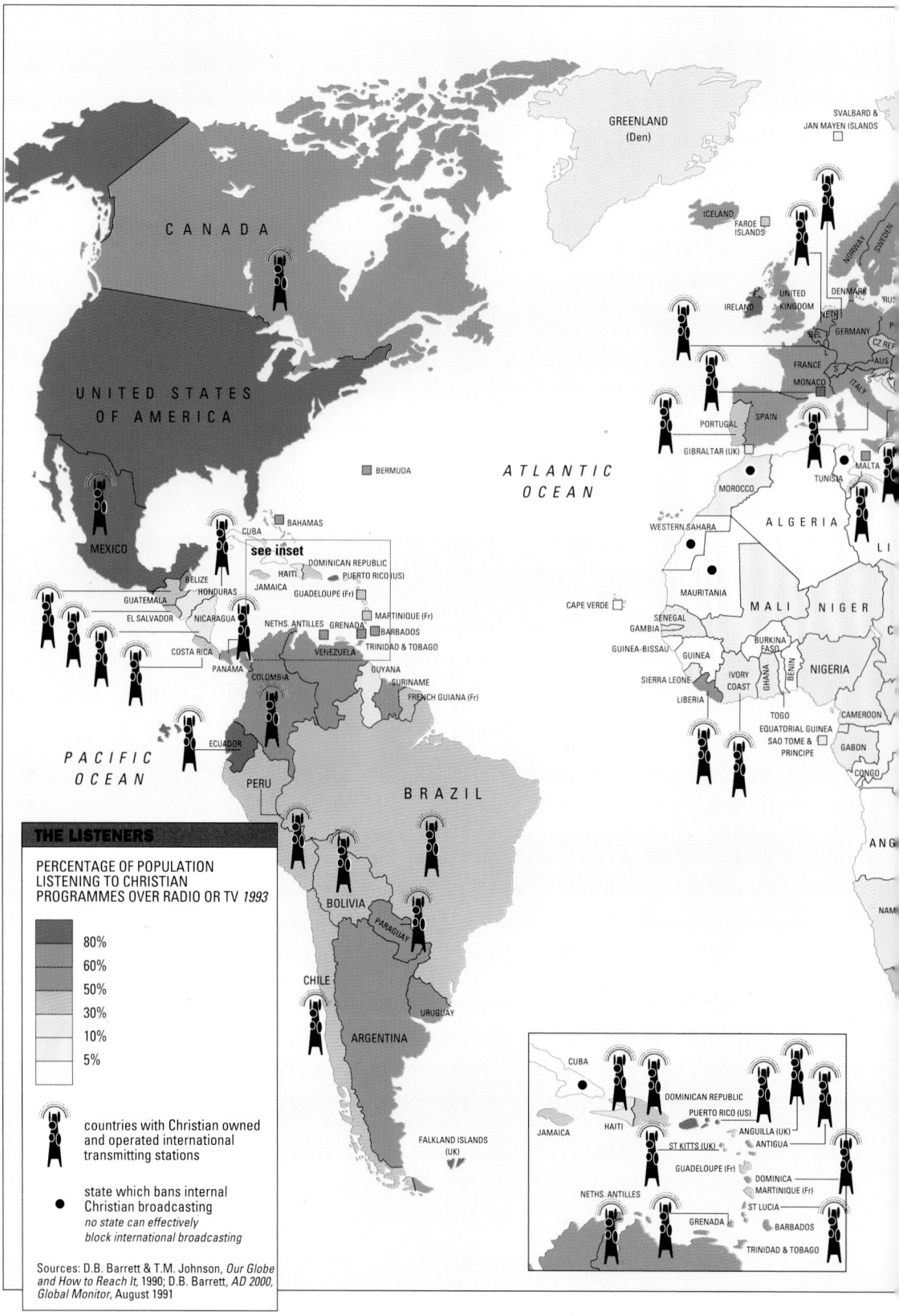

The only regular contact many Christians have with their own faith is via radio and television. While Christian broadcasting is aimed at and reaches every country in the world, 99.9 percent is produced for those where most people are already Christian.

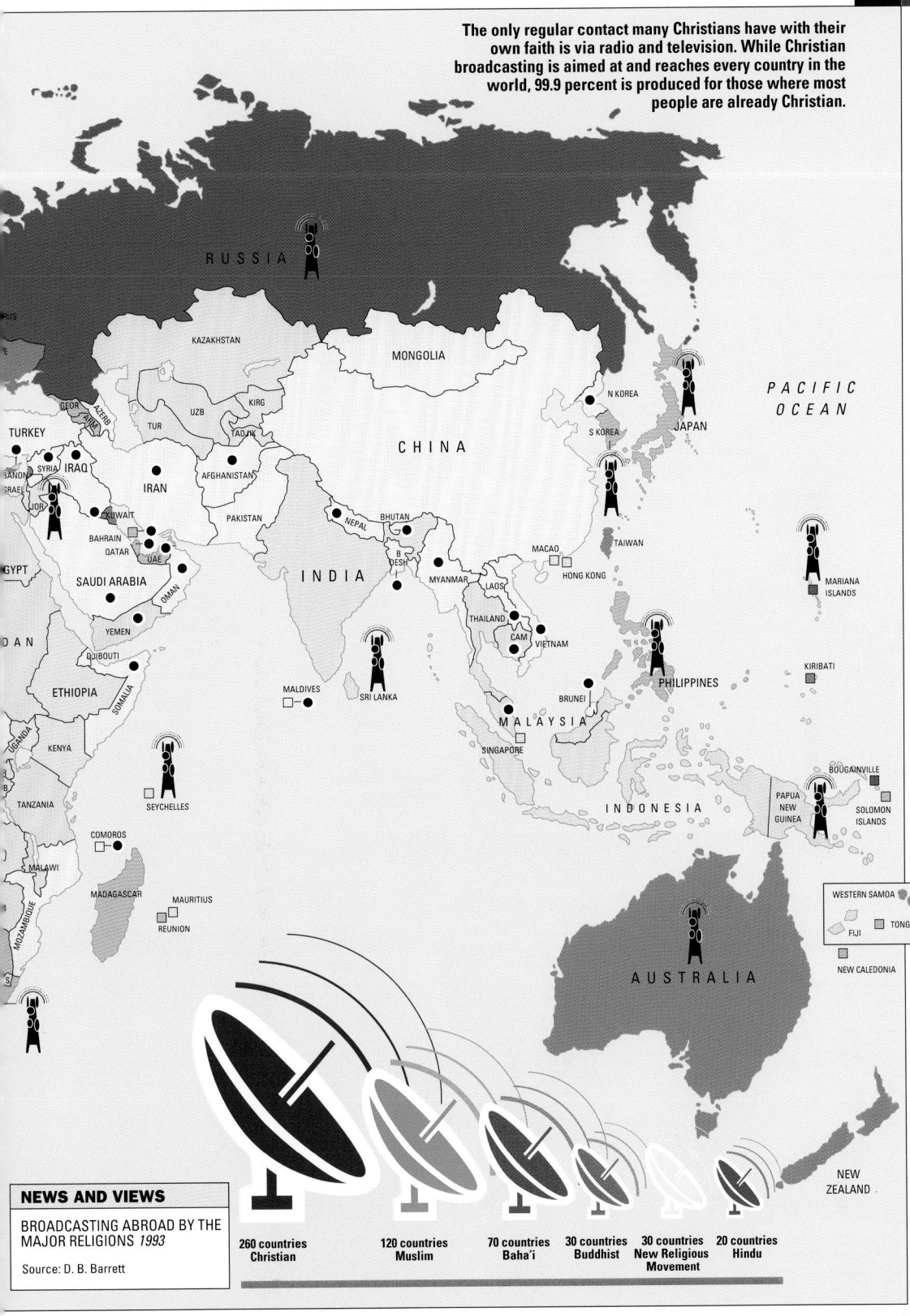

NEWS AND VIEWS

BROADCASTING ABROAD BY THE MAJOR RELIGIONS *1993*

Source: D. B. Barrett

Copyright © Myriad Editions Limited

CHRISTIAN GIVING 17

There are thousands of Christian aid agencies worldwide. These are among the largest. Aid is not usually given on the basis of religious affiliation.

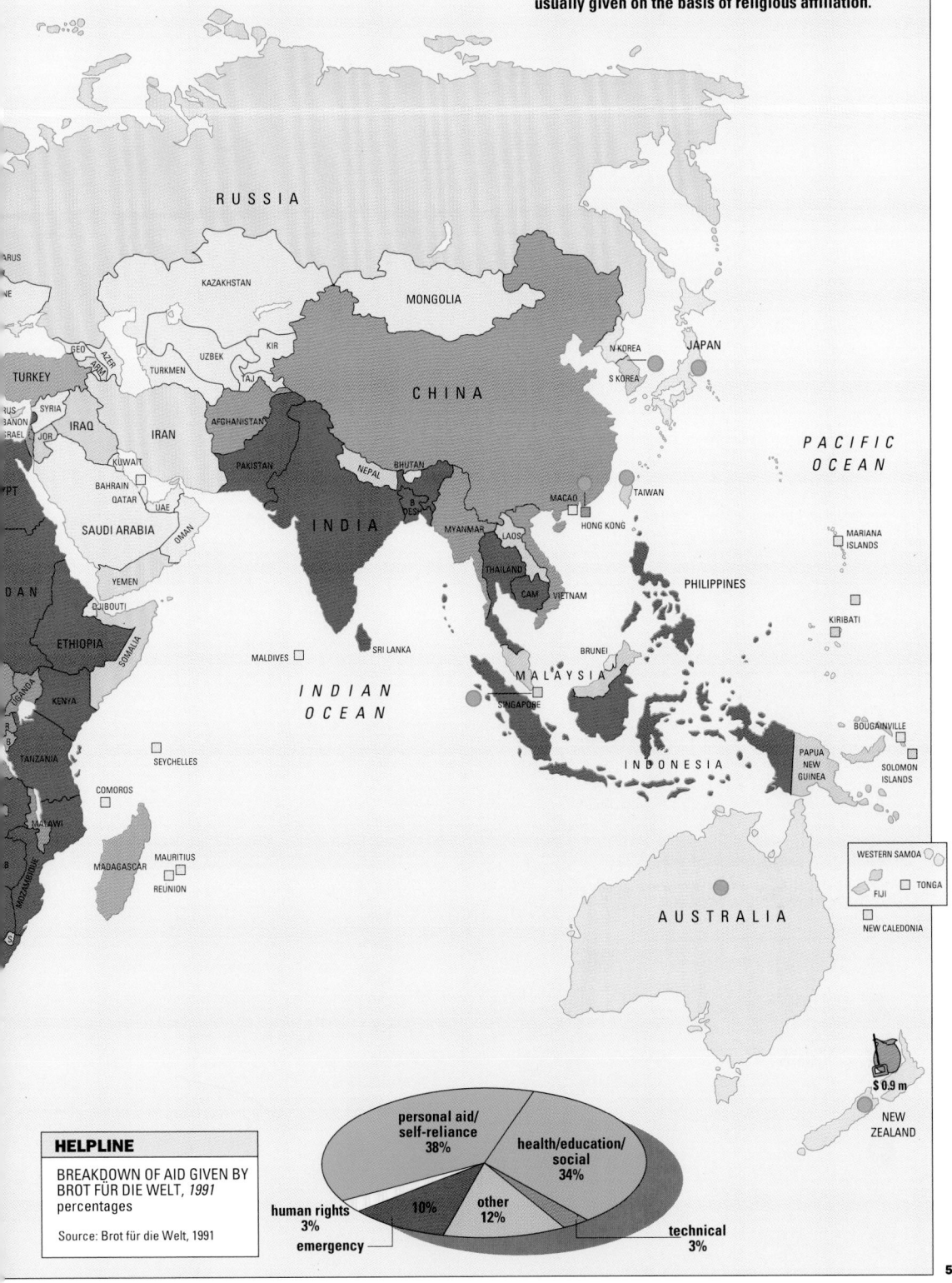

HELPLINE

BREAKDOWN OF AID GIVEN BY BROT FÜR DIE WELT, *1991*
percentages

Source: Brot für die Welt, 1991

Copyright © Myriad Editions Limited

MUSLIM GIVING 18

The giving of zakat – part of personal wealth which must be given each year for charity – is one of the Five Pillars of Islam. International Muslim aid agencies have recently emerged to fund development aid to areas of need.

Copyright © Myriad Editions Limited

The Qur'an forbids the charging and taking of interest. Some countries are working to create an Islamic non-usury form of banking. Strict application of Islamic law would mean that all trade would be by barter or exchange of precious metals. Ultimately, paper money and the whole notion of banking are alien to Islam.

Copyright © Myriad Editions Limited

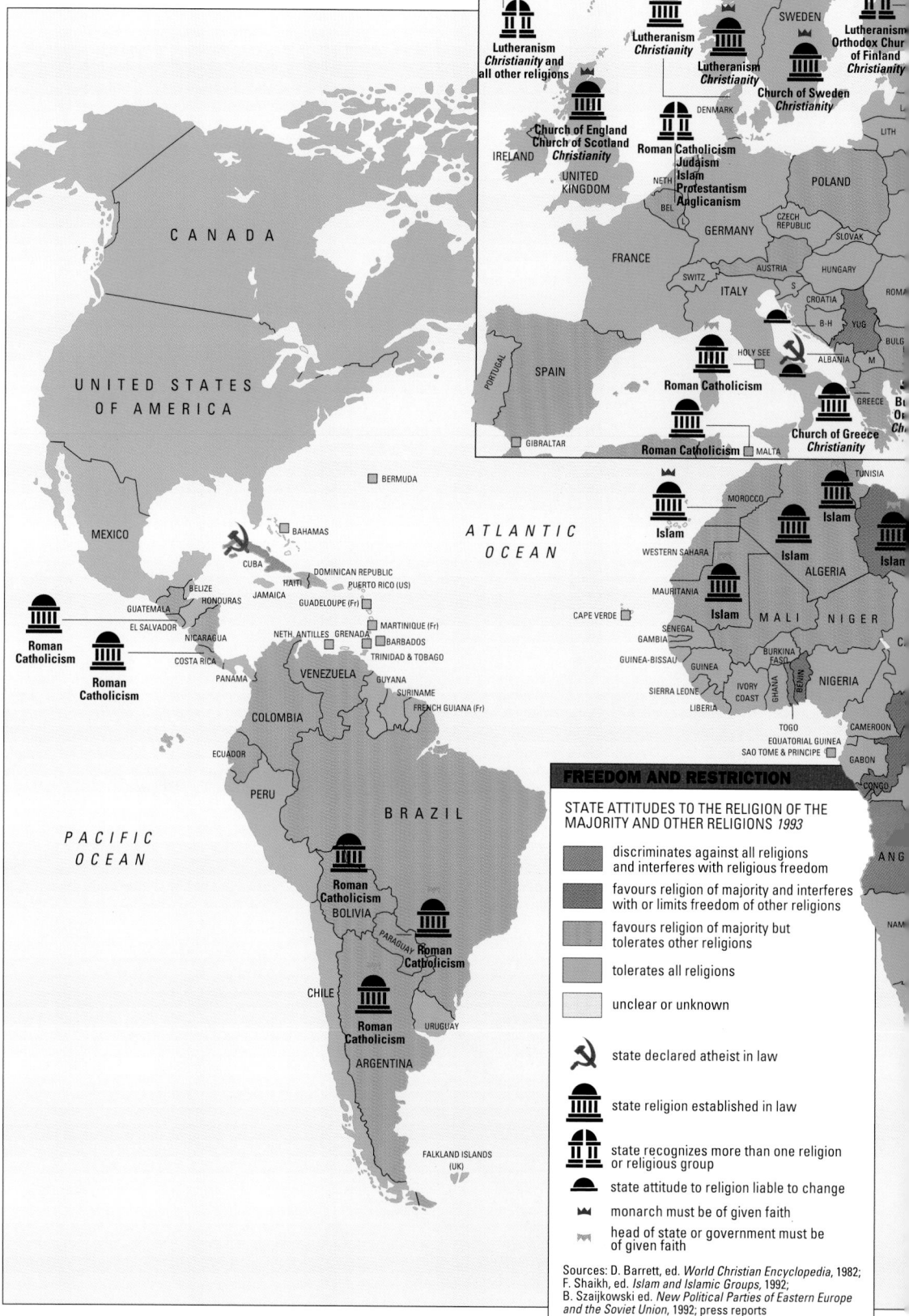

STATE FAIR - AND UNFAIR 20

Nearly a quarter of the world's states have formal links with a religion. Three states have links with more than one. A few states, including those officially atheist, actively discriminate against all religions.

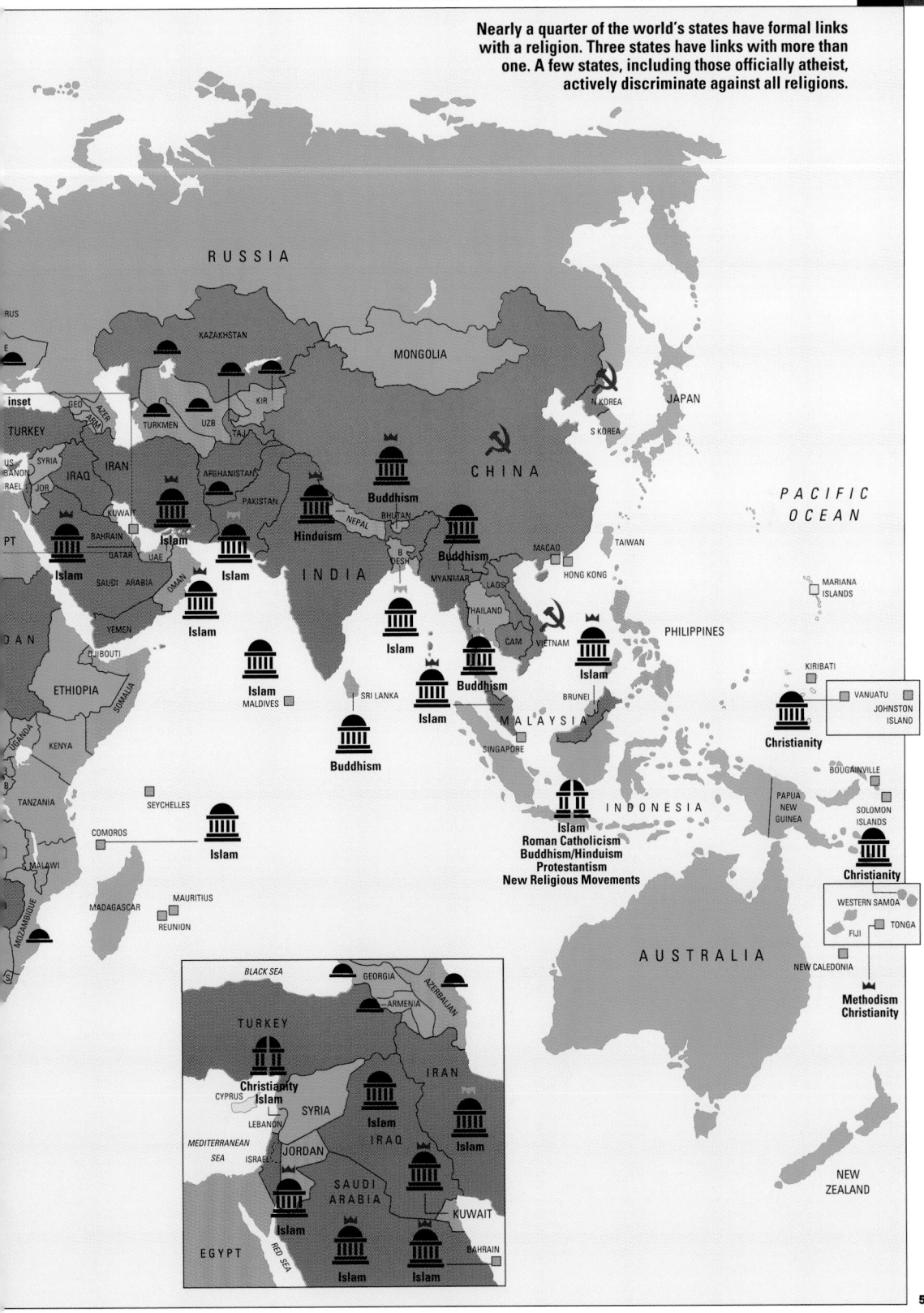

Copyright © Myriad Editions Limited

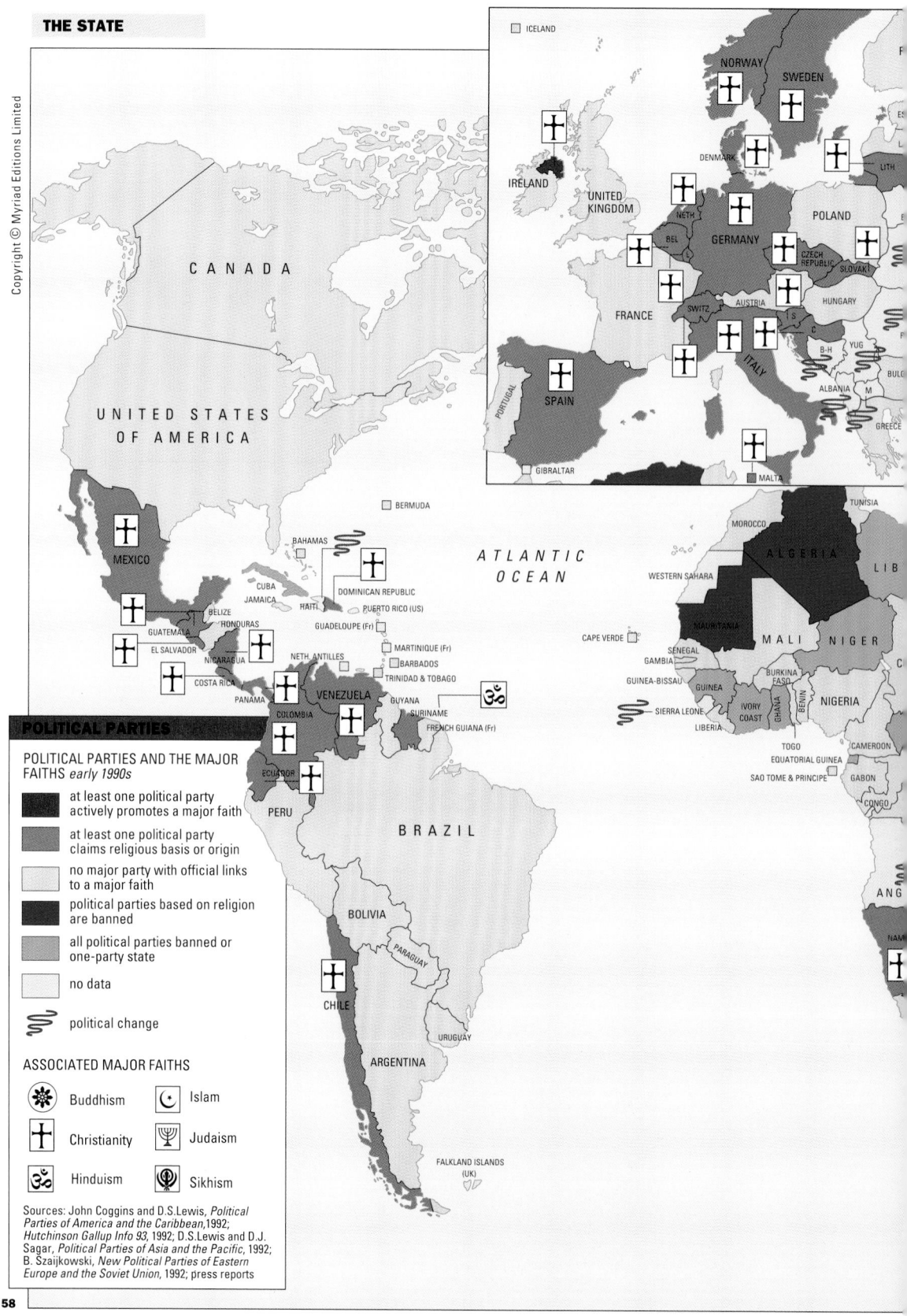

LIFE AND SOUL OF THE PARTY 21

Religion and politics do not mix, say many politicians across the political spectrum. But many parties have religious origins or links.

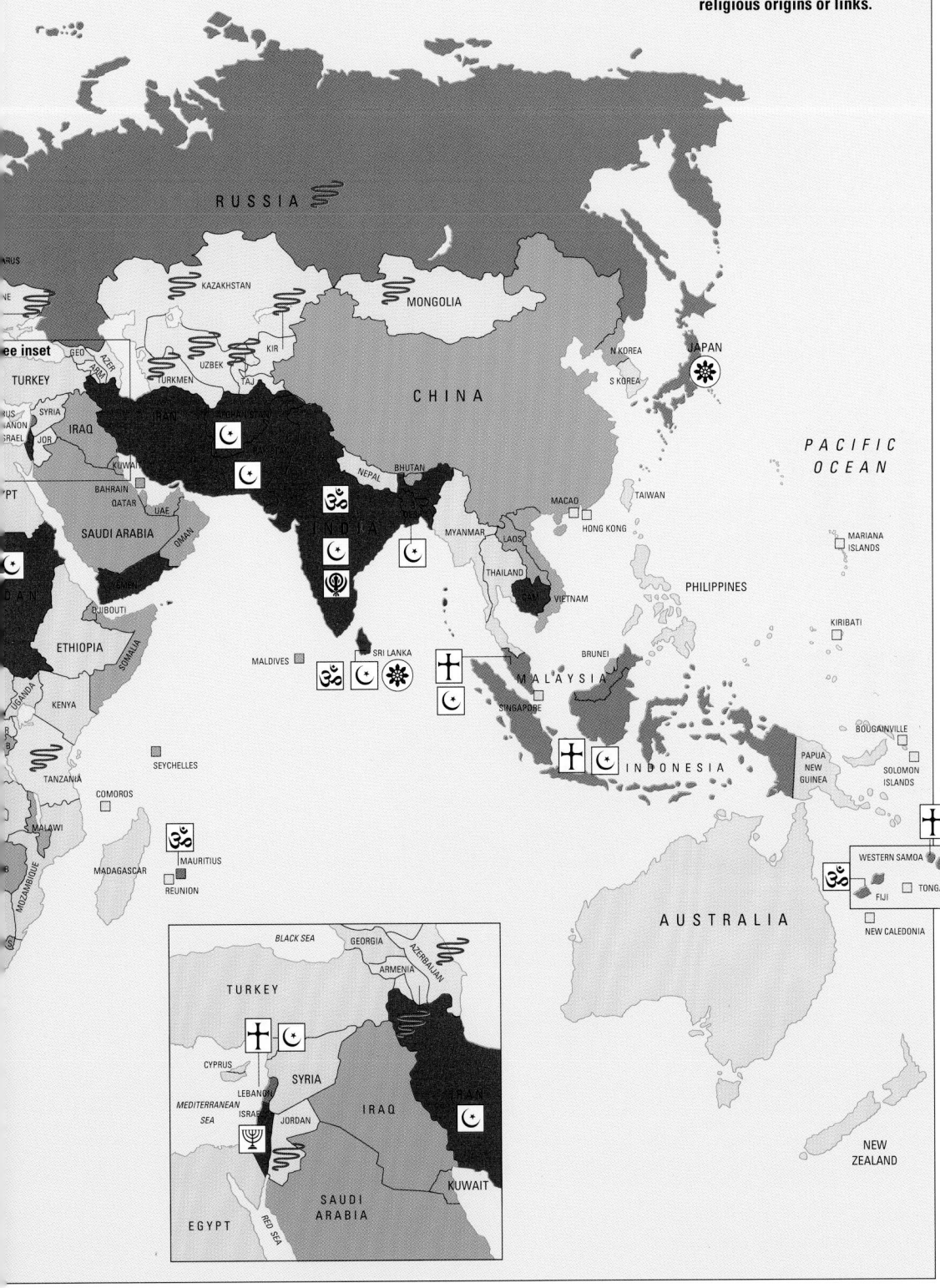

Copyright © Myriad Editions Limited

GENERATION TO GENERATION 22

As societies become multi-cultural, religious education is moving away from one of its major roles, of indoctrination into the majority faith.

Copyright © Myriad Editions Limited

GOD AND MAMMON 23

Substantial state funding, where given, goes usually to the majority faith. All states give at least minimal support: to religious charitable work, or to religious sites of national historical significance.

Copyright © Myriad Editions Limited

ISLAMIC LAW 24

The Shari'ah sets out for Muslims the basic codes, legal and ethical, upon which all relationships and institutions should be founded and by which they should be guided.

Copyright © Myriad Editions Limited

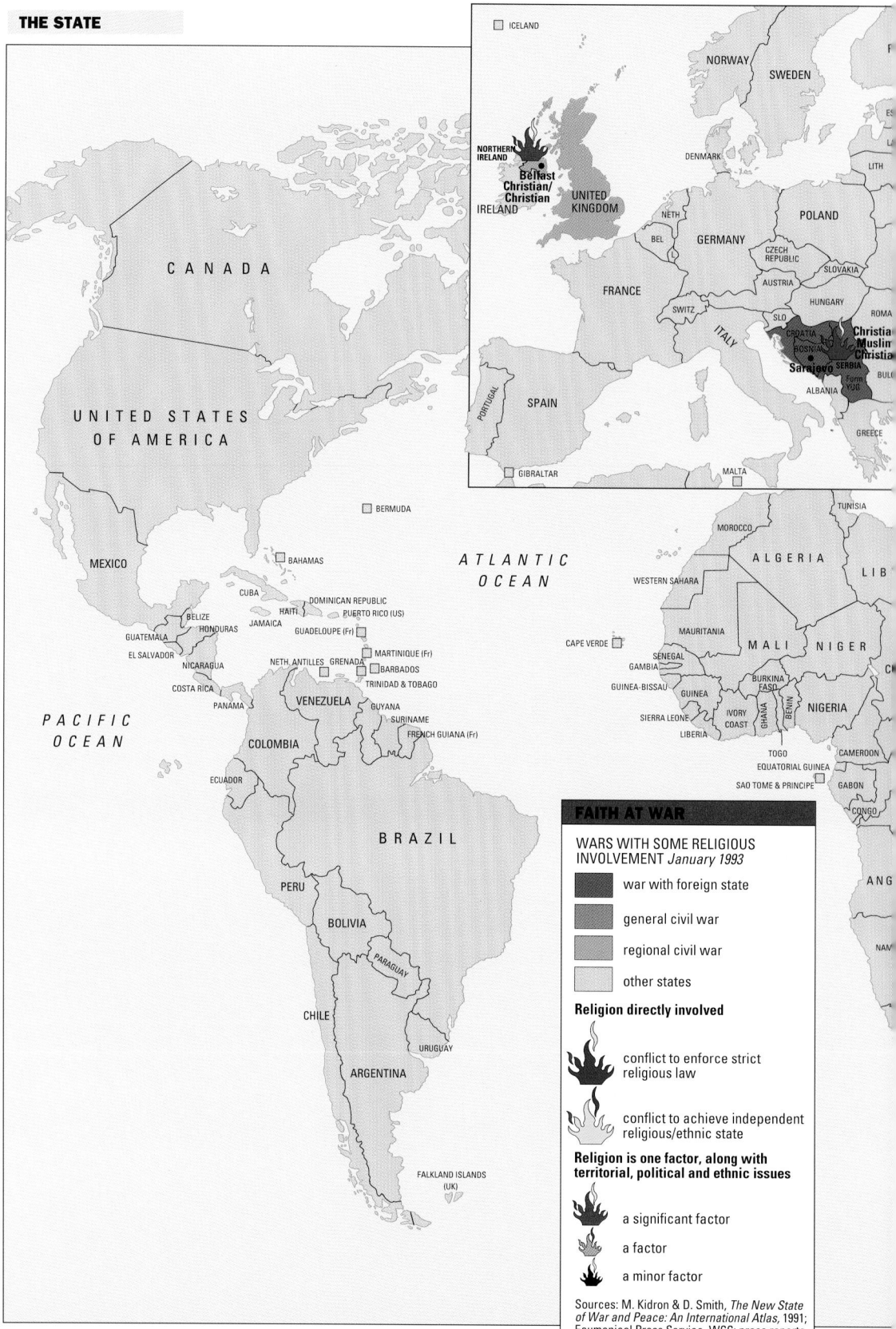

Most religions preach peace, yet the catalogue of wars in the name of religion down the ages seems to belie the claim. In the wars of the early 1990s, religion is rarely the major factor but its role is increasing.

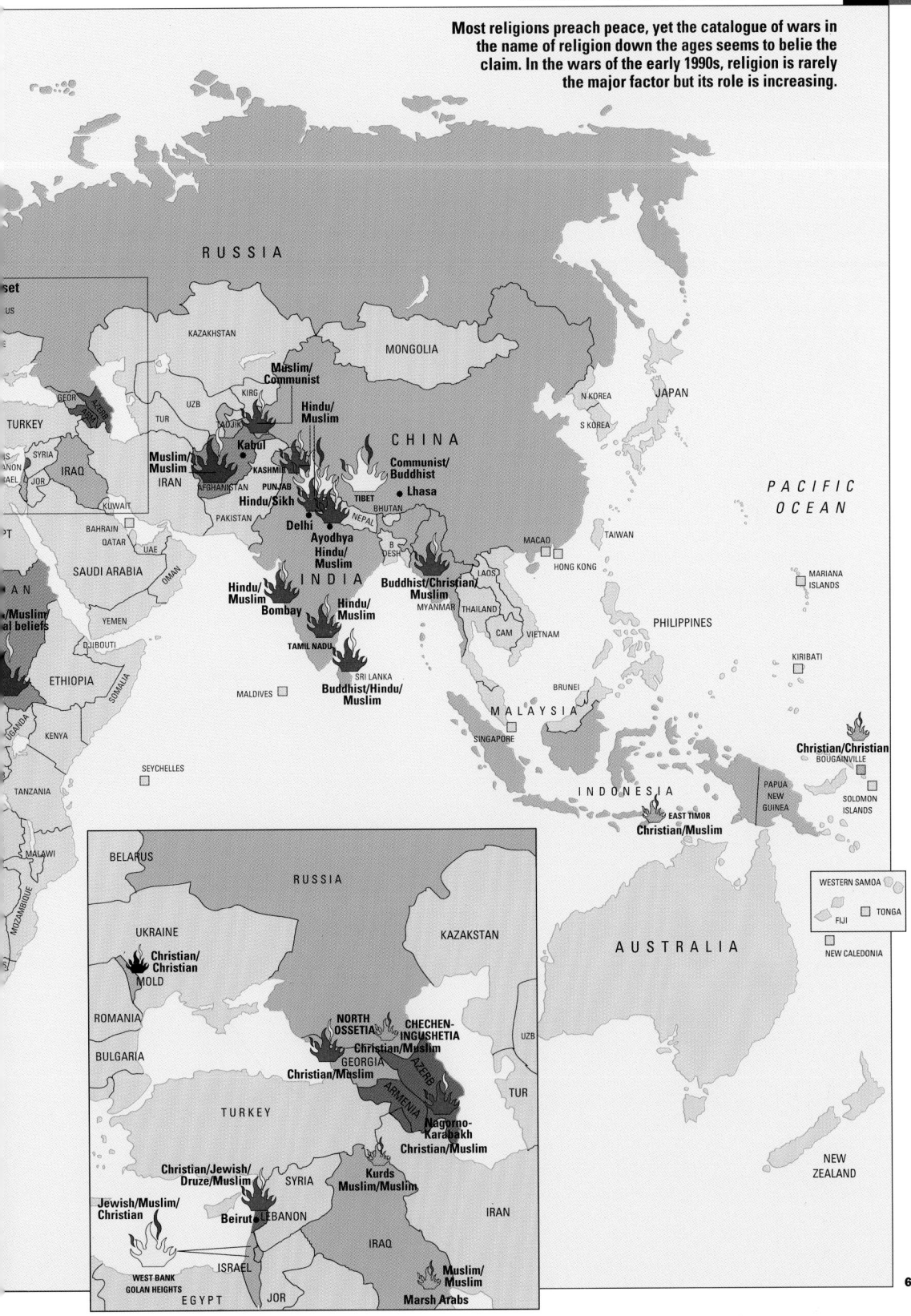

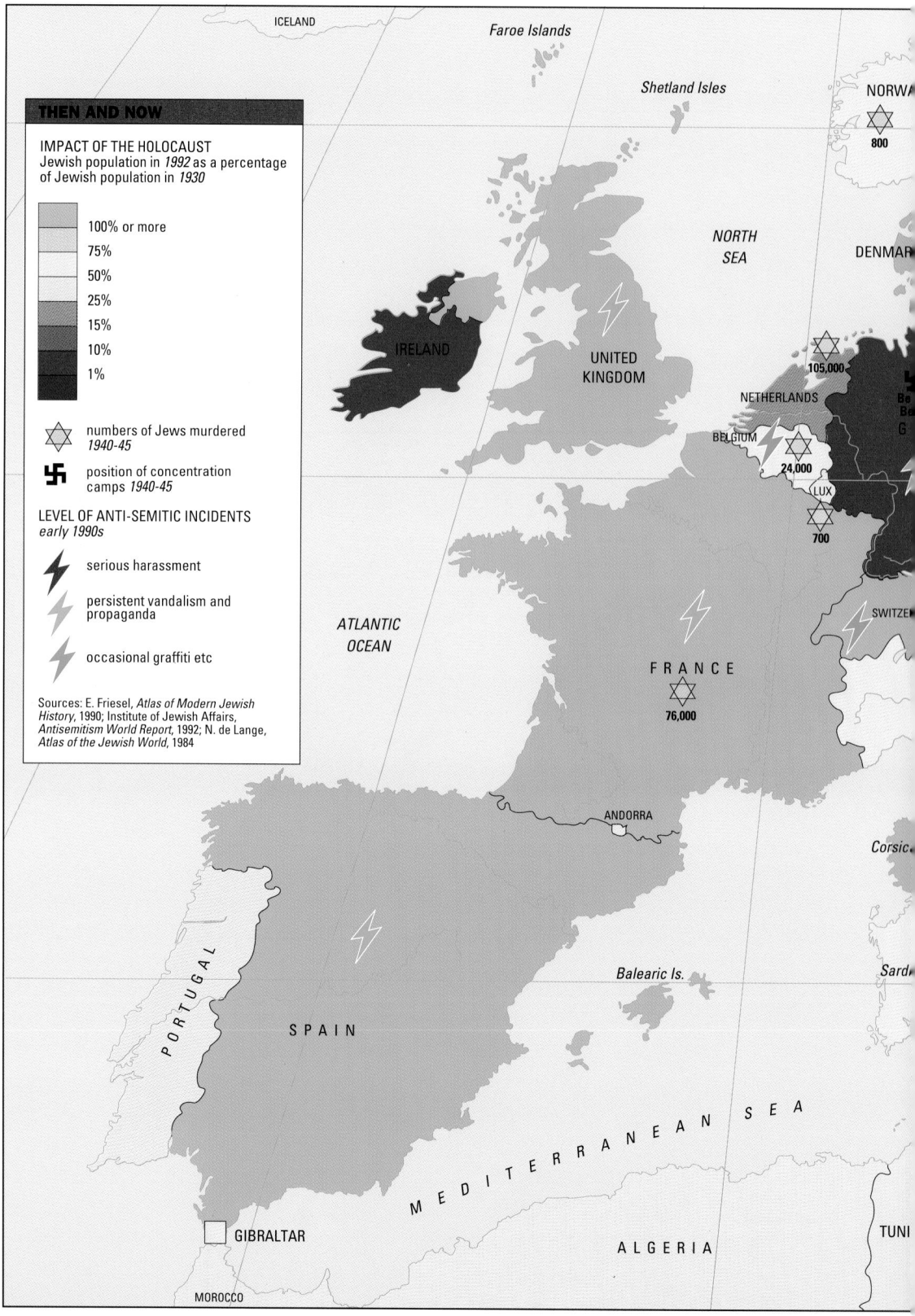

Copyright © Myriad Editions Limited

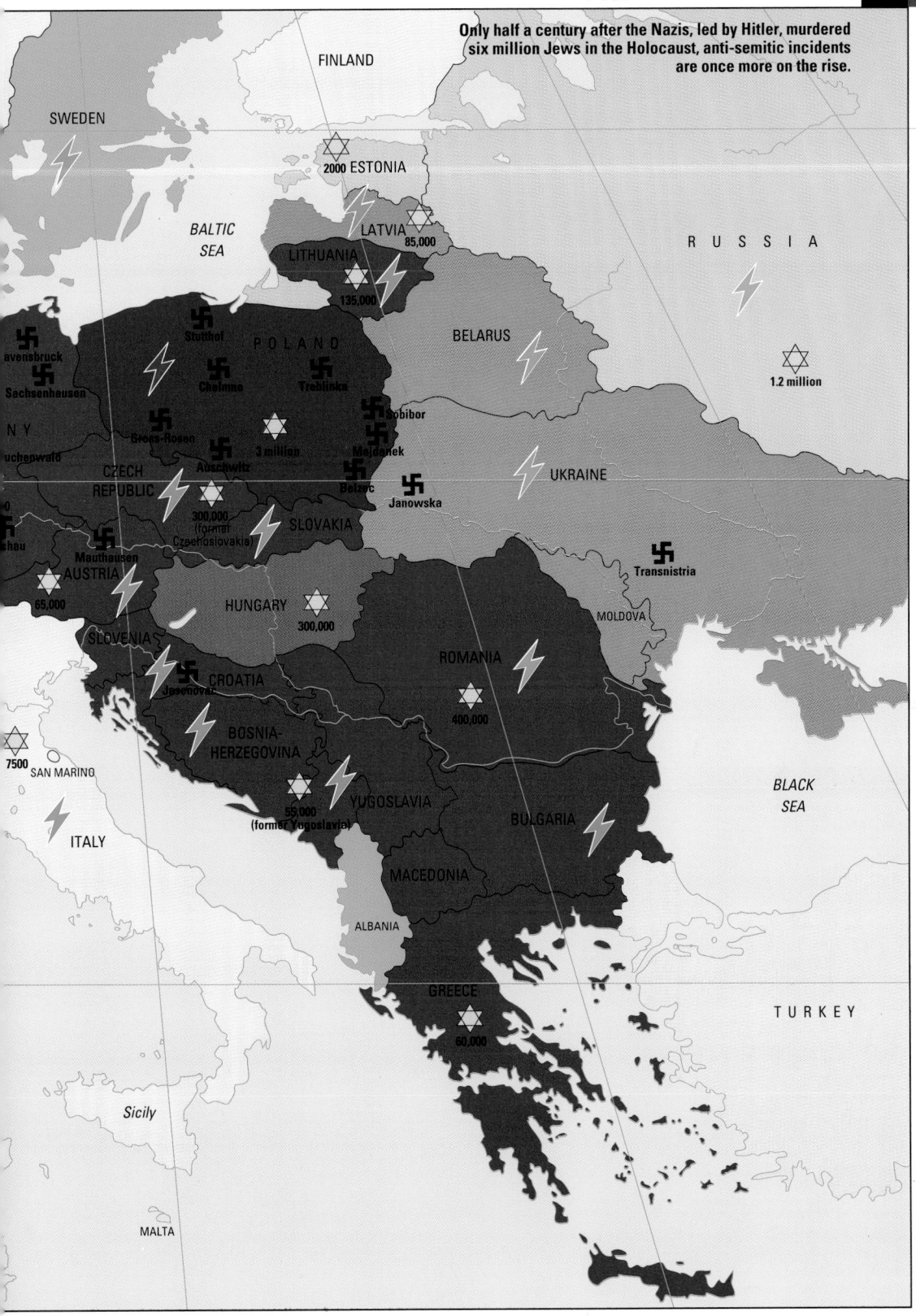

Only half a century after the Nazis, led by Hitler, murdered six million Jews in the Holocaust, anti-semitic incidents are once more on the rise.

Copyright © Myriad Editions Limited

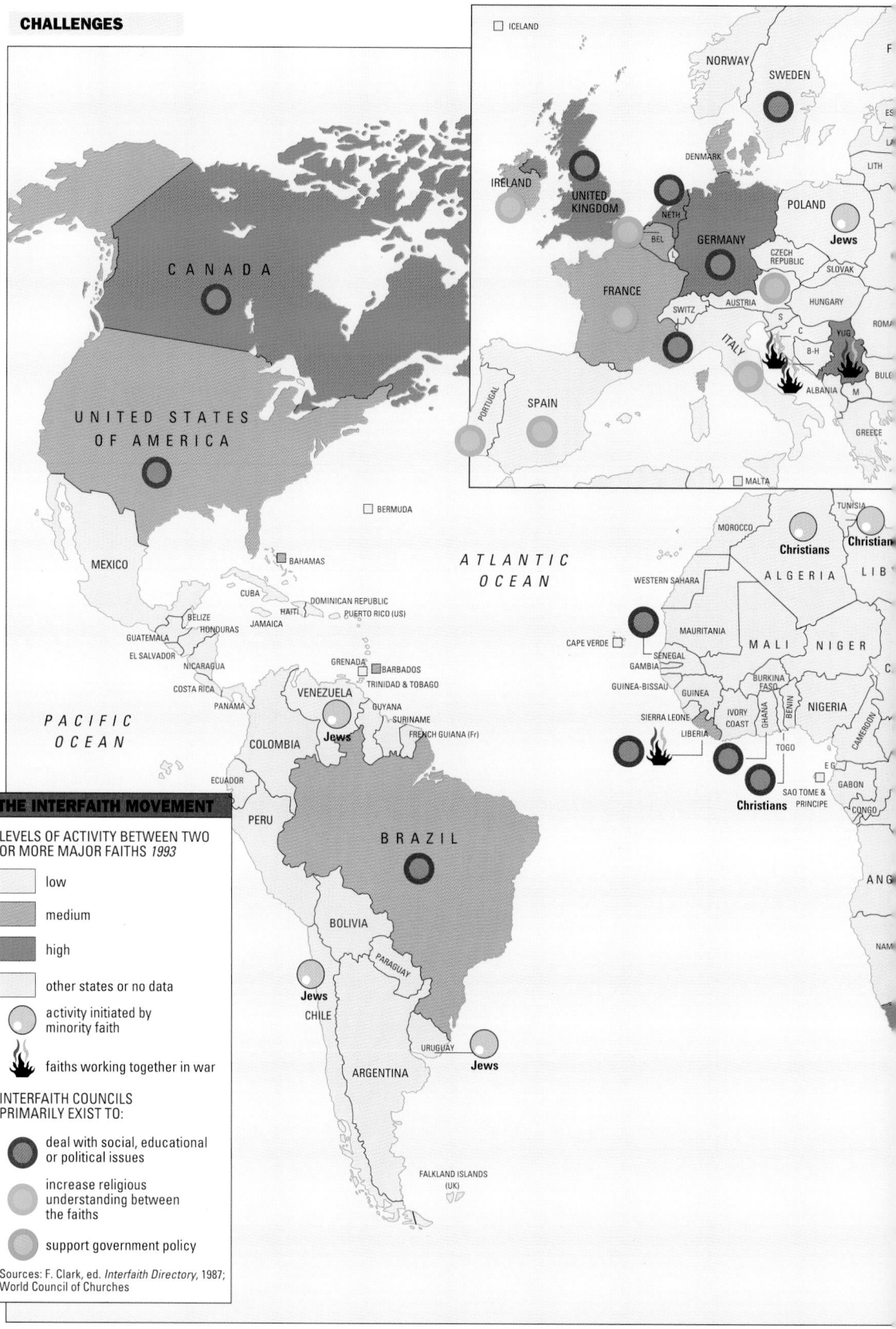

FAITH TO FAITH 27

After a century of effort the interfaith movement is still limited. Religions sometimes work together over social or political problems. Often, minority faiths seek to form links which will give them recognition.

Copyright © Myriad Editions Limited

THE ECUMENICAL MOVEMENT 28

There has been a drive towards a united Christian church since the beginning of the century. There have been some reunion schemes, notably in non-Christian majority countries, but there are now more Christian denominations than ever.

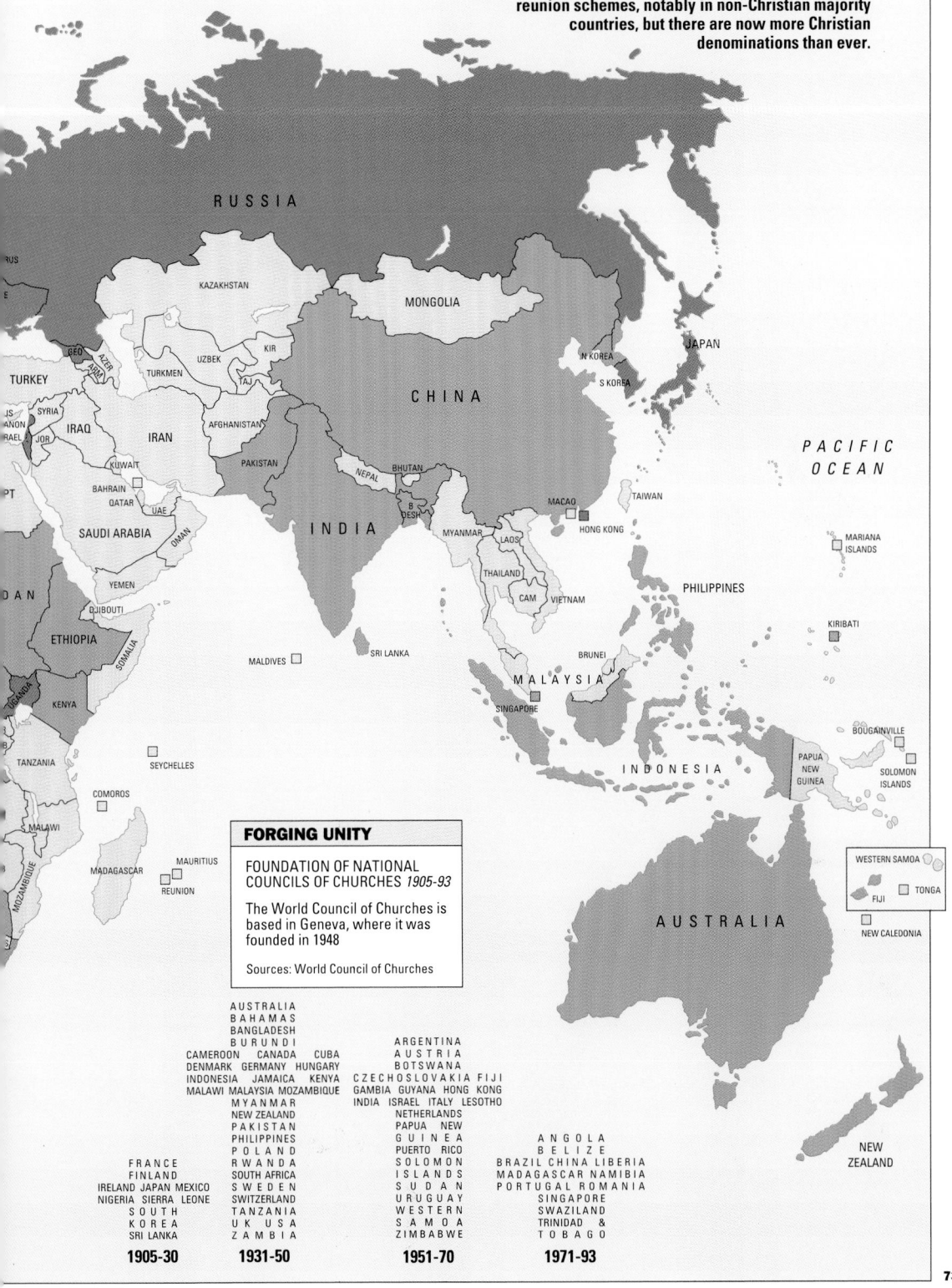

FORGING UNITY

FOUNDATION OF NATIONAL COUNCILS OF CHURCHES *1905-93*

The World Council of Churches is based in Geneva, where it was founded in 1948

Sources: World Council of Churches

1905-30
FRANCE
FINLAND
IRELAND JAPAN MEXICO
NIGERIA SIERRA LEONE
SOUTH KOREA
SRI LANKA

1931-50
AUSTRALIA
BAHAMAS
BANGLADESH
BURUNDI
CAMEROON CANADA CUBA
DENMARK GERMANY HUNGARY
INDONESIA JAMAICA KENYA
MALAWI MALAYSIA MOZAMBIQUE
MYANMAR
NEW ZEALAND
PAKISTAN
PHILIPPINES
POLAND
RWANDA
SOUTH AFRICA
SWEDEN
SWITZERLAND
TANZANIA
UK USA
ZAMBIA

1951-70
ARGENTINA
AUSTRIA
BOTSWANA
CZECHOSLOVAKIA FIJI
GAMBIA GUYANA HONG KONG
INDIA ISRAEL ITALY LESOTHO
NETHERLANDS
PAPUA NEW GUINEA
PUERTO RICO
SOLOMON ISLANDS
SUDAN
URUGUAY
WESTERN SAMOA
ZIMBABWE

1971-93
ANGOLA
BELIZE
BRAZIL CHINA LIBERIA
MADAGASCAR NAMIBIA
PORTUGAL ROMANIA
SINGAPORE
SWAZILAND
TRINIDAD & TOBAGO

Copyright © Myriad Editions Limited

The women's movement has forced some religions to give women equal status and rights. Other religions claim that feminism is a 'Western' issue and irrelevant to their faith.

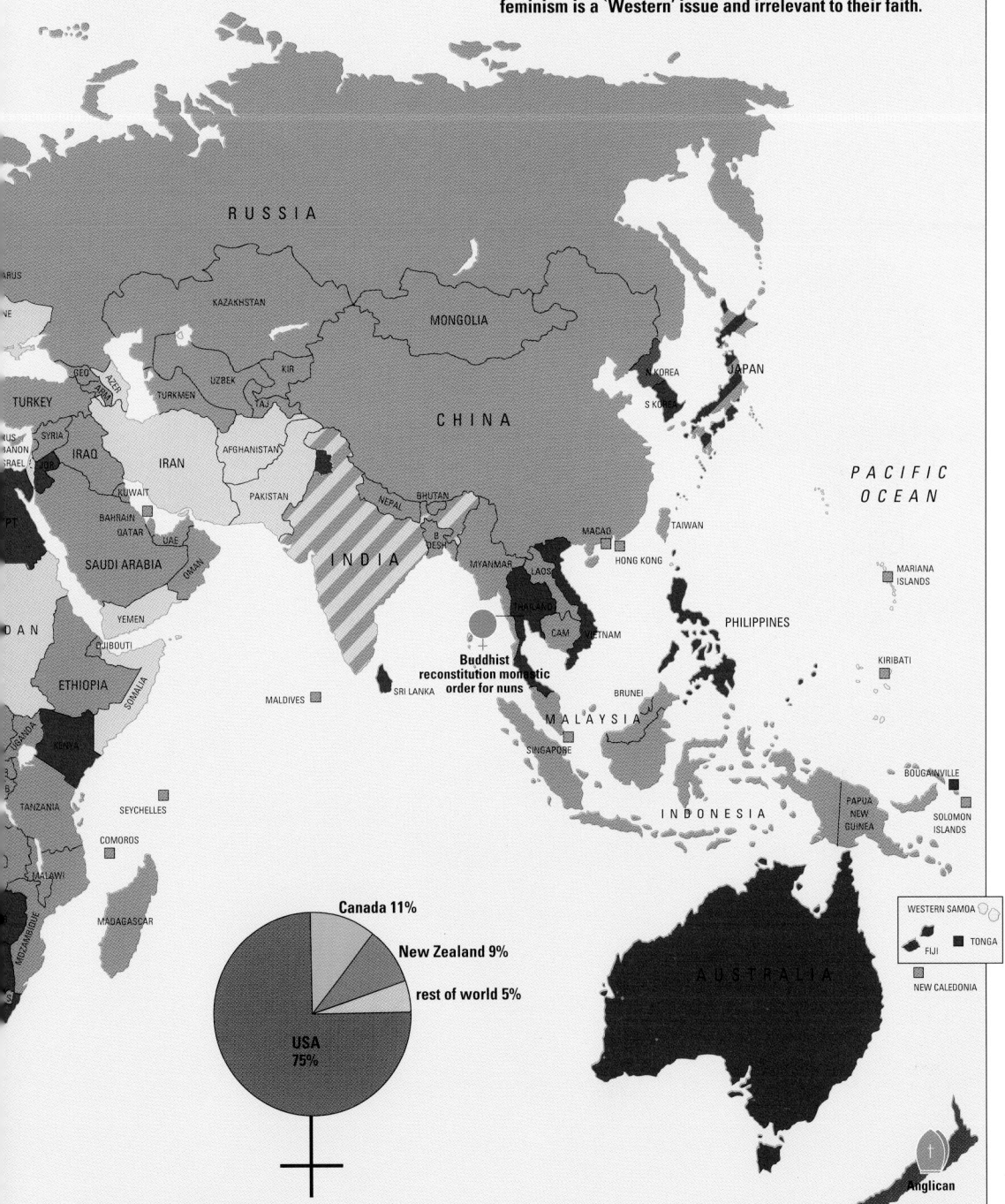

ORDINATION OF WOMEN

SHARE OF WOMEN PRIESTS IN THE ANGLICAN COMMUNION *1992* percentages	Number of women priests by province or jurisdiction World total: 1381
Source: Anglican Consultative Council, London	USA 1031; Canada 158; New Zealand 120; Uganda 36; Australia 10; Ireland 7; Brazil 5; Southern Africa 3, West Africa 3; Burundi 2, Hong Kong 2, North India 2; Kenya 1, Philippines 1, South India 1

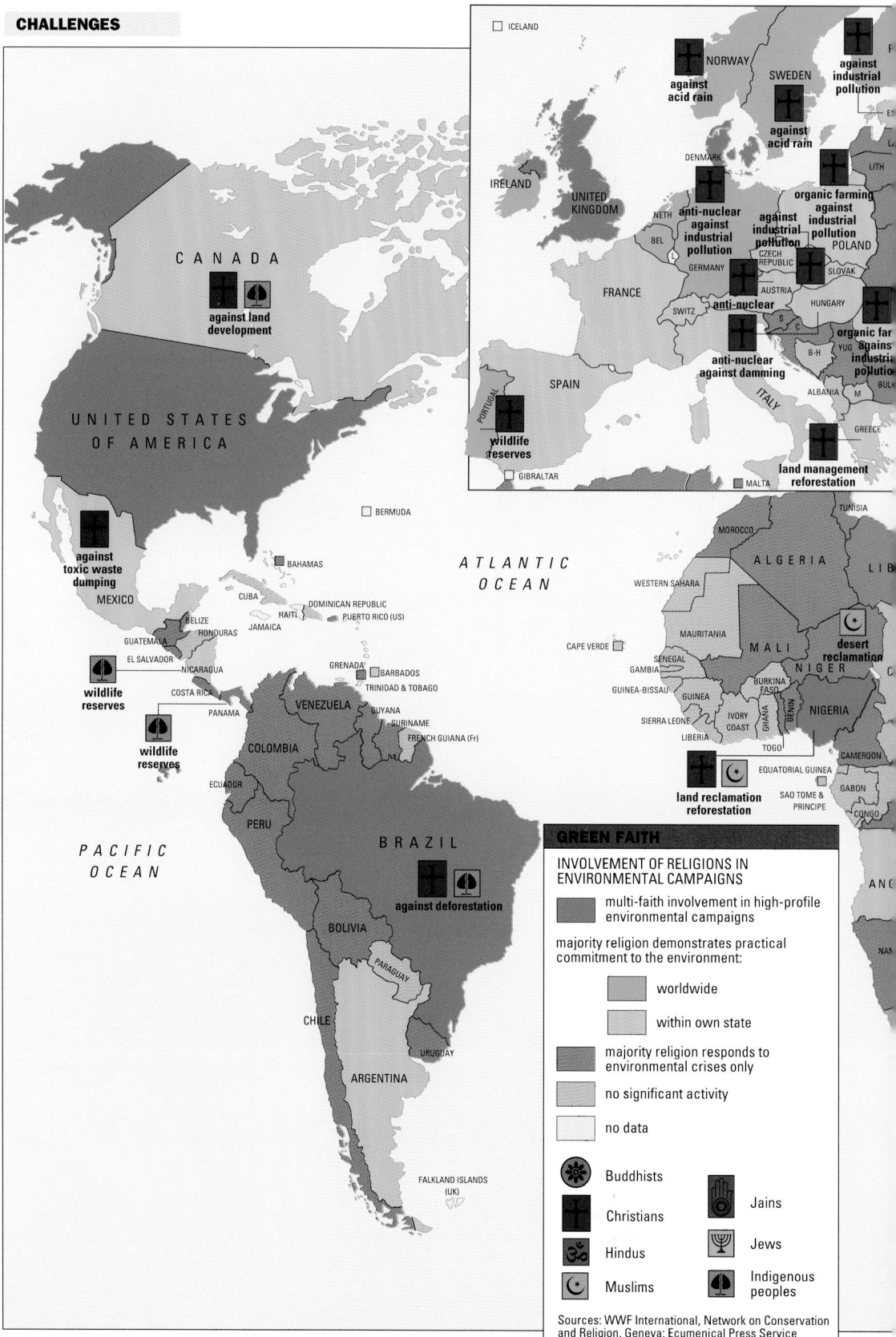

Copyright © Myriad Editions Limited

DOWN TO EARTH 30

The environmental crisis has provoked the religions into a major re-examination of their basic teachings and beliefs. They are now taking significant action worldwide, often working together.

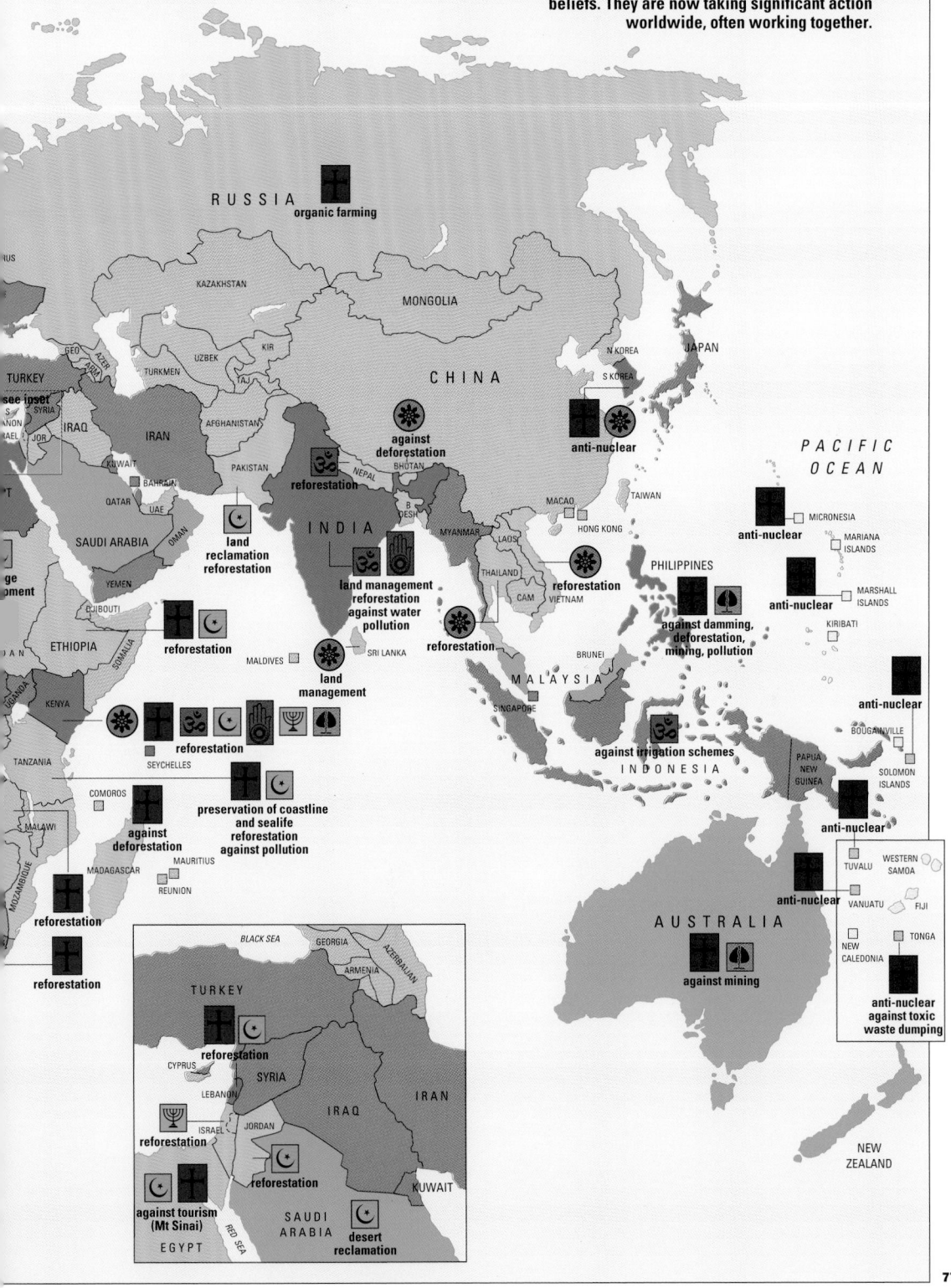

Copyright © Myriad Editions Limited

There will be a worldwide increase in religious allegiance, intensity and diversity. In some countries this will lead to further religious tension.

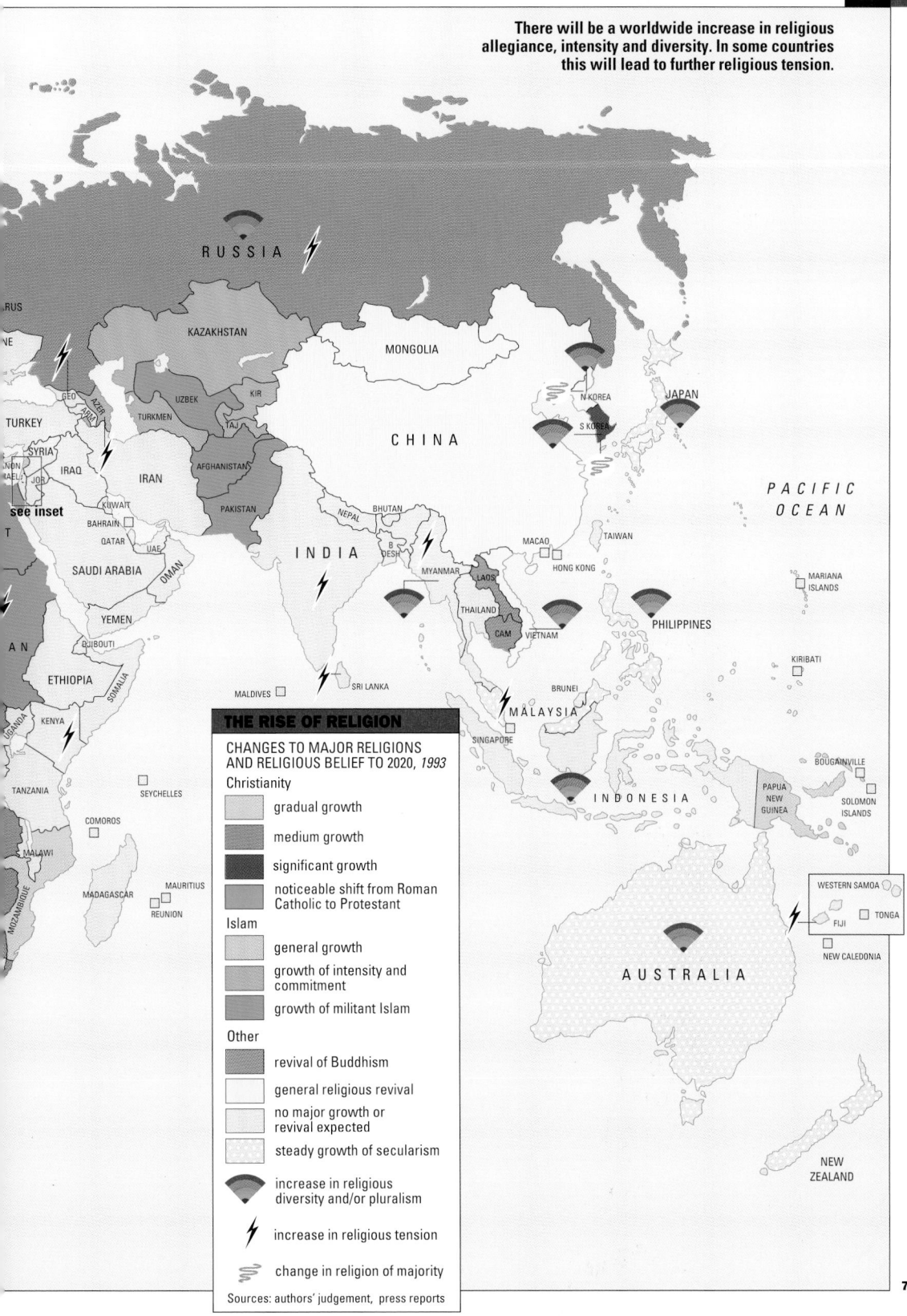

Part 3

THE HEARTLANDS

Copyright © Myriad Editions Limited

Places associated with where the faiths began or where major new expressions came to life are often centres of pilgrimage and veneration.

Copyright © Myriad Editions Limited

THE HAJJ

PLACE OF ORIGIN OF PILGRIMS TO MAKKAH *1987*

total: 960,386 pilgrims

Sources: Saudi Information Office, London; Kingdom of Saudi Arabia, Ministry of Finance and National Economy, *Statistical Yearbook 1987*

URBAN PILGRIMAGE CENTRES

MAJOR CITIES AND TOWNS HOLY TO ONE OR MORE WORLD RELIGION

Major tourist centres:

founded or built as a holy city *date*

later became a holy city

other Holy cities or towns:

founded or built as holy *date*

later became holy

site of religious tension

Sources: Aubrey Rose; Ranchor Prime; Iftikhar Awan; Mawil Izzidien; Rupert Gethin

Holy cities often attract many tourists – religious and non-religious. A few cities are holy to more than one faith. Jerusalem is holy to three. Every Muslim will try to visit Makkah at least once.

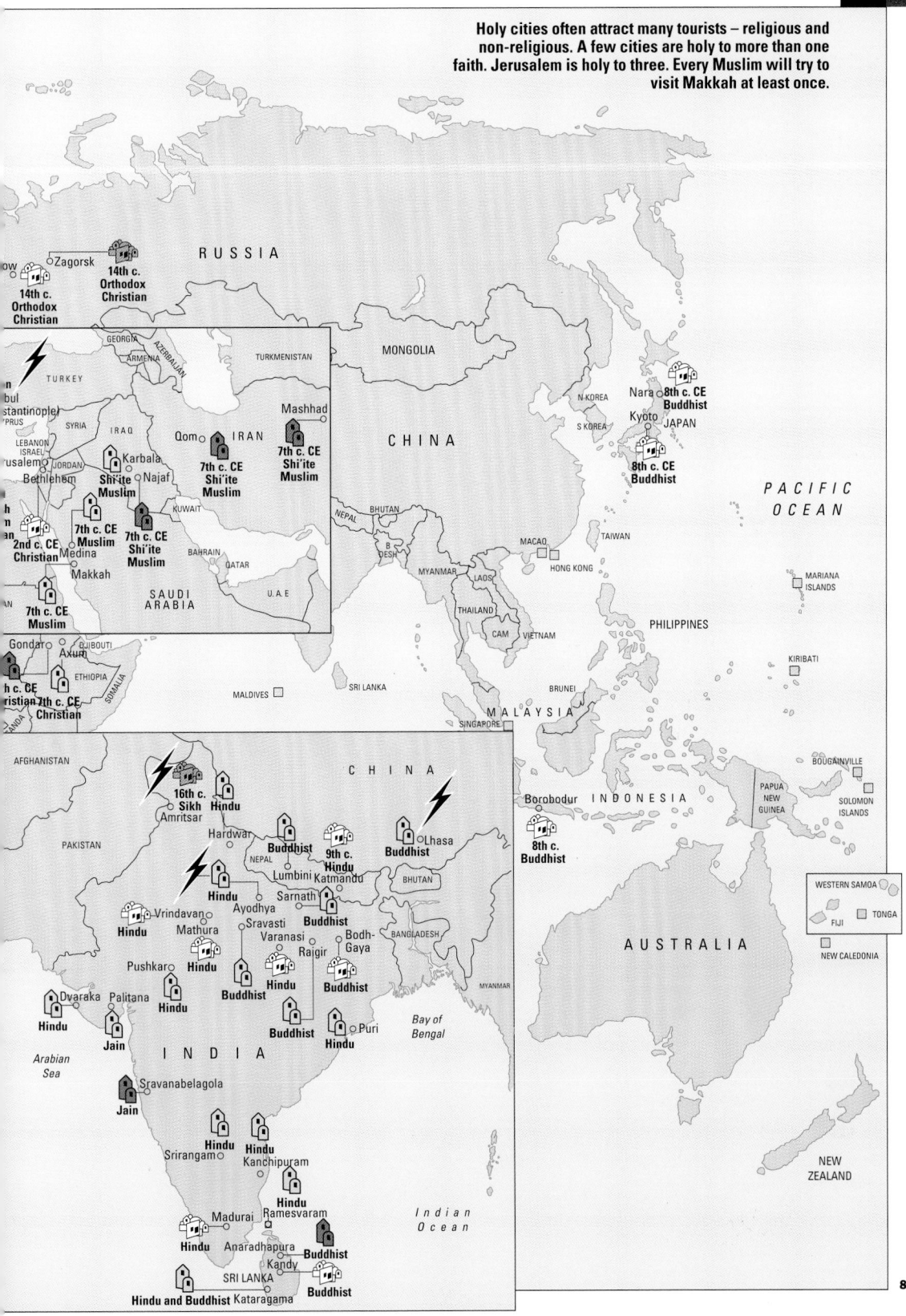

Copyright © Myriad Editions Limited

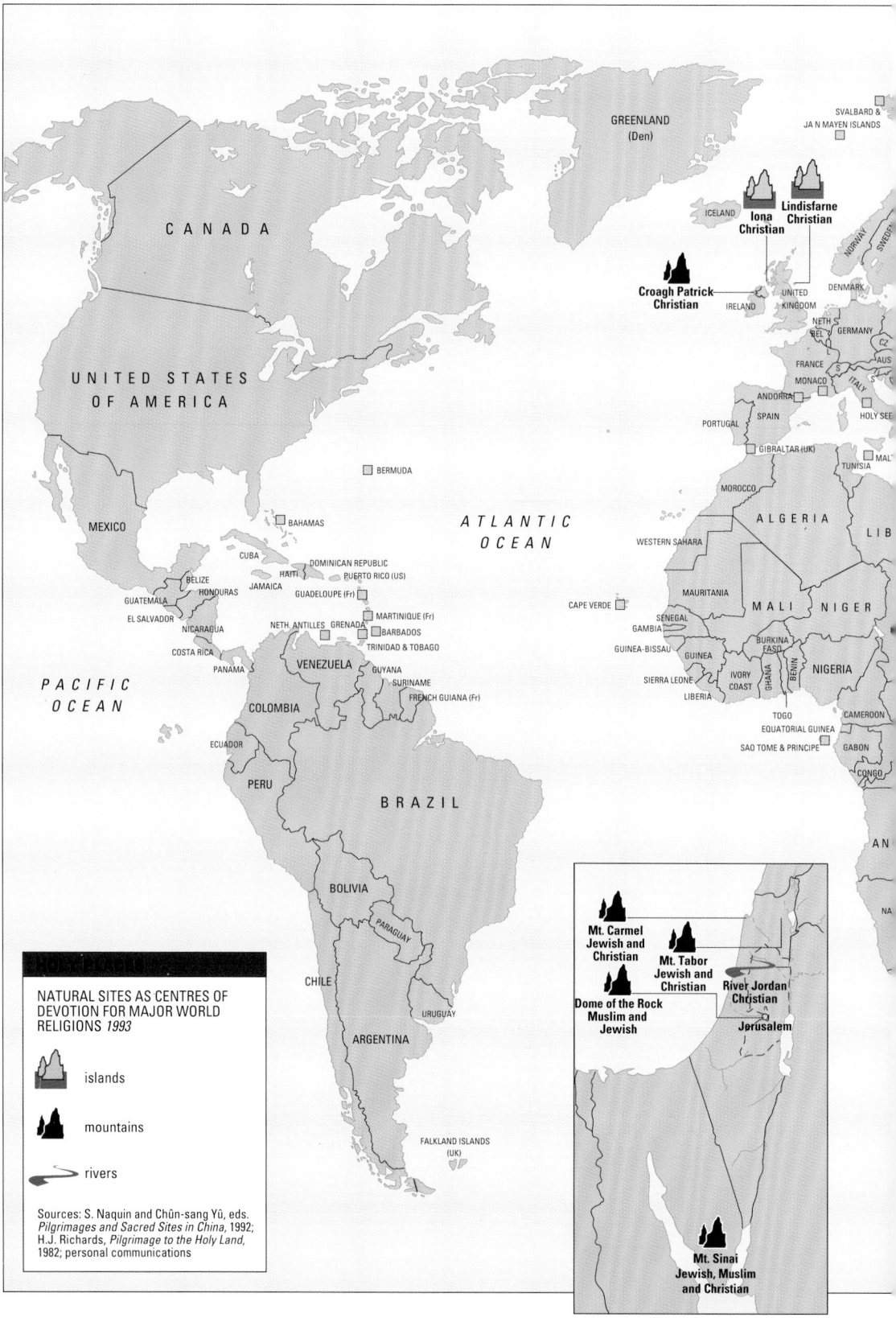

Some elements of landscape are revered not just for their beauty, but for their association with a key religious figure or event.

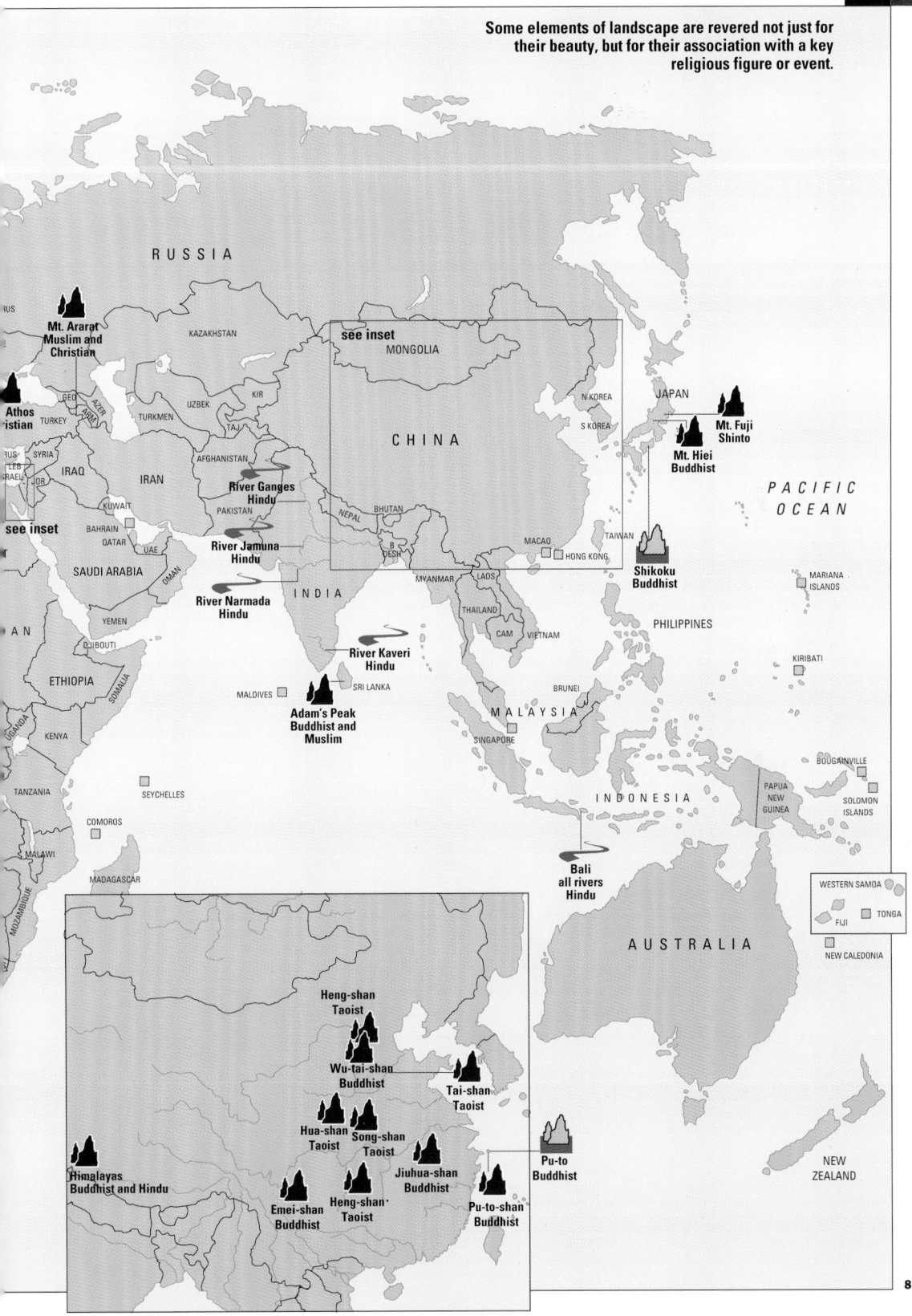

FUNDAMENTALS OF THE FAITHS

THE NATURE OF GOD

BUDDHISM

Buddhists generally recognize the existence of 'supernatural' or god-like beings, but do not believe in an omnipotent creator God. All Buddhists recognize a transcendent truth and some conceive this in terms of a 'Buddha Nature' which infuses everything.

CHRISTIANITY

Christians believe in one God, creator of all things, considered to be three 'persons', the Trinity: God the Father, the Son (Jesus Christ) and the Holy Spirit.
These three aspects of God co-exist within one Godhead.

HINDUISM

Hindus believe in one Godhead or Divine Power, with innumerable forms. Three major forms are: Brahma, creator of each universe; Vishnu, sustainer and defender; and Shiva, destroyer and re-creator. Vishnu has ten main forms or avatars which come to the help of the universe. These include Krishna and Rama.

ISLAM

Muslims believe there is one God, Allah. (Arabic for God). Allah is indivisible, has no equals, is the creator of all and has spoken to humanity through many prophets, of whom Muhammad is the last.

JUDAISM

One God (whose name must not be pronounced), who created all things and who through his special covenant with the Jews has guided human life and destiny.

SIKHISM

One God, who is the true Guru (teacher). Unbound by time or space and beyond human definition, he makes himself known to those who are ready.

TAOISM

Taoists believe in universal forces of nature – yin and yang. Through creative tension with each other they keep the world spinning and moving. Popular Taoism has thousands of gods but Taoists do not believe in a single supreme God.

THE CREATION

BUDDHISM

For Buddhists the Creation is cyclical, having no start and no end. It is part of the wheel of suffering to which we are attached through re-birth. Creation is seen as just part of this wheel.

CHRISTIANITY

All that exists does so through God who began creation at a definite point in time and who will end creation. God created from nothing and all that he creates has purpose and meaning.

HINDUISM

Creation is cyclical. From the destruction of a previous universe, Brahma arises to create a new universe; Vishnu sustains it through a cycle of birth, growth and decline; Shiva destroys the universe and the cycle begins again.

ISLAM

God is the creator. He simply says 'Be' and all things exist. God guides his creation and has a purpose for all forms of life within creation.

JUDAISM

God is the creator and the Book of Genesis says he created in six days and rested on the seventh. God will end creation in his own time.

SIKHISM

God is the creator of all, so all life is good. Attachment to this world means rebirth, so that release from this world is the highest goal.

TAOISM

Creation as an event is not of great importance. There are various stories. In essence, the twin forces of yin and yang were created from nothing rather than by any being, and from these twin forces come all life.

TIME

BUDDHISM

Time is cyclical. Each existence continues through death and rebirth so long as the sense of self keeps us attached to this world. Individual desires are finally quenched (nirvana) but the world continues on its cyclical pattern. Some forms of Buddhism believe in a future Buddha who will come and bring release to all beings.

CHRISTIANITY

Time is linear, though there are two very different approaches. In one, there is the suggestion that through human lives a renewed and peaceful world will be created – the Kingdom of God on earth. In the second, the world becomes so full of suffering and wrongdoing that an antichrist will appear, bringing conflict. Christ then returns and defeats the antichrist in a great battle inaugurating a reign of peace.

HINDUISM

Time is cyclical. The world passes through various stages, from birth to growth to decline. We are currently in Kali Yuga, the age of decline. The world will eventually be destroyed, only for a new world to appear in the distant future.

ISLAM

Time is linear. At the end of time, God will announce the Judgement Day and the world will end. All will be judged on that day.

JUDAISM

Time is linear. The Messiah, or the Chosen One of God, will come when either the world has become a better place or when it has reached the point of greatest trouble. The Messiah will herald an era of world peace.

SIKHISM

Time is cyclical and beliefs associated with time are similar to those of Hinduism.

TAOISM

There are elements of both the linear and the cyclical.There is no end to the world, just a personal journey, either to better and better rebirths, or into immortality.

LIFE AFTER DEATH

BUDDHISM

At death, each life continues in some other form – human, divine or animal, depending upon the results of behaviour in the last life. The goal of Buddhism is to extinguish the flame of wanting or attachment to the sense of self so that rebirth does not occur and Nirvana is attained.

CHRISTIANITY

There is one life only. Beliefs about death vary. The soul may ascend to heaven and be judged by God; or, the soul and the body may be raised on the Day of Judgement , at the end of time, and will then be judged.

HINDUISM

Depending upon the karma – the consequences of action in this present life – at death, the soul (atman) is reborn in either a higher or lower physical form. Through devotion or correct behaviour it is possible to ascend through the orders of reincarnation, achieve liberation from the cycle of rebirth, and be reunited with the Supreme Being.

ISLAM

There is one life only. After death, the individual awaits the Day of Judgement when all will be brought back to life and judged. Paradise awaits those who have lived according to the will of God and those who have failed to do so cannot enter Paradise.

JUDAISM

There is one life only. Most religious Jews believe the individual awaits the Day of Judgement when God will raise all to life and judgement. Some, however, believe that the soul is judged immediately after death.

SIKHISM

Each individual has many reincarnations, but being born a human means the soul is nearing the end of rebirth. God judges each soul at death and may either reincarnate the soul or, if pure enough, allow it to rest with him.

TAOISM

At death, the soul is judged by up to 10 different gods of Hell, is purified by punishment then reborn again. Certain schools believe death is avoidable. By practising special meditations or eating certain things, the body is made immortal so that the person lives forever.

SACRED LITERATURE

BUDDHISM

The teachings of the Buddha are handed down in a collection of writings known as the 'Three Baskets' (*Tri-Pitaka*), comprising the discourses of the Buddha, the rules of discipline for Buddhist monks and nuns, and further knowledge – the 'great teaching basket'. Three versions survive: one in the Pali language (used by southern Buddhists) and two Mahayana versions in Chinese and in Tibetan (used by northern Buddhists). The Mahayana versions include later books not recognized as authoritative by southern Buddhists.

CHRISTIANITY

The Bible consists of the Old Testament – the books of the Hebrew Bible – plus the New Testament. The books of the New Testament were fixed c. 280 CE and are the Gospels, Acts of the Apostles, letters from writers such as Paul and James and the Book of Revelation.

HINDUISM

There are many sacred books, of which the Bhagavad Gita and the Upanishads are seen as the most important.

ISLAM

The Qur'an, dictated by the Angel Jibra'il to Muhammad in the first part of the 7th century CE. Muslims believe the Qur'an was written by God before time began.

JUDAISM

The Hebrew Bible has three parts. The Torah (Five Books of Moses), the Prophets and the Writings such as Esther and the Psalms. The Torah contains laws, doctrine and guidance on way of life, as well as accounts of the early history of the Jewish people and their relationship with God.

SIKHISM

The Guru Granth Sahib, a collection of writings and hymns by some of the 10 Gurus of Sikhism, plus material from Muslim and Hindu writers. It was compiled mid-16th century and was made the eleventh and final Guru of Sikhism at the death of the tenth Guru in 1708.

TAOISM

There are over 4000 books in the Taoist Canon, from the 4th century BCE to the 14th century CE. Each school has its own favourites and many look back to the Tao Te Ching of Lao Tzu, compiled c. 4th century BCE, as their initial source of inspiration.

PROPHETS AND FOUNDERS

BUDDHISM

The Buddha was an Indian Prince, Siddhartha Gotama, who lived in the 5th century BCE. He became known as the Enlightened One (Buddha) when he understood the cause of suffering and the way to end suffering.

CHRISTIANITY

The faith is named after Jesus Christ, who was born in Palestine c. 4 BCE and crucified c. 29 CE. Christians believe he is the Son of God, part of the Trinity and that he came to earth in human form to bring humanity back to fellowship with God.

HINDUISM

There are thousands of Hindu gurus, reflecting the huge variety of teachings. A guru, or teacher, is someone who has gained enlightenment through knowledge and practice. A Hindu wanting to follow a particular path of prayer, meditation and devotion usually has a guru.

ISLAM

Islam means to be in submission to God, who is seen as its founder. There have been numerous prophets who came to remind people of God's will, such as Abraham, Moses and Jesus. The final prophet is believed to be Muhammad who lived in the 6th–7th century CE.

JUDAISM

Through the covenant with Abraham and his descendants, God chose the Jews as his special people. This covenant was reaffirmed and consolidated with Moses, when God gave Moses the Law by which Israelites were to live.

SIKHISM

Guru Nanak (1469–1539) was the first Guru of Sikhism and was followed by nine more human Gurus. The tenth and last was Guru Gobind Singh (1675–1780), who appointed the Scriptures, the Granth Sahib, as the final Guru.

TAOISM

There have been various figures, ranging from mythical emperors to semi-historical figures such as Lao Tzu (5th century BCE) and Chang Tao Ling (2nd century CE), who founded popular Taoism.

RITES OF BIRTH AND DEATH

BUDDHISM

Buddhists invite monks and nuns to attend such events and to read the scriptures, but the main ceremonies are generally from older traditions. In Theravada Buddhism, funerals are occasions for teaching about suffering and impermanence and for chanting *paritta* (protection) in order to gain and transfer merit for the sake of the deceased.

CHRISTIANITY

Many Christians are baptized into the Church while they are babies, but this can be done at any time in life. At death, Christians are laid to rest in the hope of the resurrection of the dead. Cremation or burial are both acceptable.

HINDUISM

Before birth and in the first months of life, there are many ceremonies. These include: reciting the scriptures to the baby in the womb; casting its horoscope when it is born; cutting its hair for the first time. At death, bodies are cremated and the ashes thrown on to a sacred river. The River Ganges is the most sacred river of all.

ISLAM

At birth, the call to prayer is whispered into the baby's ear. After seven days the baby is given a name, shaved, and baby boys are circumcized. At death, the body is washed as if ready for prayer and then buried as soon as possible. Cremation is not allowed.

JUDAISM

Baby boys are circumcized eight days after birth. The names of girls are announced in the synagogue on the first Sabbath after birth. Burial takes place within 24 hours of death and cremation is very rare. The family is in full mourning for seven days and, for eleven months, the special prayer Kadish is said every day.

SIKHISM

At birth, the Mool mantra, the core teaching of Sikhism, is whispered into the baby's ear. The baby is named at the gurdwara, or place of worship. The Guru Granth Sahib is opened and the first letter of the first word on the page gives the first letter of the baby's name. At death, the body is cremated and the ashes thrown on to running water.

TAOISM

Horoscopes are cast at birth. After a month a naming ceremony is held. At death, the body is buried and paper models of money, houses and cars are burnt to help the soul in the afterlife. After about 10 years the body is dug up and the bones buried again in an auspicious site.

FESTIVALS

BUDDHISM

Wesak celebrates the life of the historical Buddha (May–June). Dhammacakka celebrates the Buddha's first sermon where he taught the principles of Buddhism (July).

CHRISTIANITY

The main festivals celebrate the life of Jesus Christ: Christmas, celebrating his birth (25 December); Easter, marking his death and resurrection (March–April); Ascension Day, celebrating his return to Heaven (May). Pentecost celebrates the coming of the Holy Spirit onto the Disciples (May–June).

HINDUISM

There are many festivals, of which the main ones are: Mahashivaratri celebrating Shiva (February–March); Holi, the harvest festival in honour of love and of Krishna (March–April); Divali, celebrating the New Year and Rama and Sita, central figures ofThe Ramayana, a Hindu epic (October–November).

ISLAM

The Muslim calendar is lunar and moves 11 days earlier each year, compared with the Western solar calendar. The months given here are for 1993–95. Ramadan is the month of fasting (February); Eid ul Fitr marks the end of Ramadan and the giving of the Qur'an to Muhammad (March); Eid ul Adha is the time of the Hajj, the pilgrimage to Makkah and celebrates the obedience of the Prophet Ibrahim (May–June).

JUDAISM

Passover or Pesach celebrates the exodus of the Jews from Egypt (March–April); Shavuot, or Pentecost, marks the giving of the Law to Moses (May–June); Rosh Hashanah is the New Year festival, and Yom Kippur, the day of repentance (both in September–October); Hanukkah celebrates the survival of the Jews (December).

SIKHISM

Baisakhi celebrates the foundation of the Khalsa (13 April); other major festivals include the Martyrdom of Guru Arjan Dev (May–June); the birthday of Guru Nanak, the founder of Sikhism (November); the Martyrdom of Guru Tegh Bahadur (November); and the birthday of Guru Gobind Singh (December).

TAOISM

There are hundreds of local festivals. The main festivals: Chinese New Year (January–February); Ching Ming, for the veneration of the dead (4 or 5 April); the Hungry Ghosts' festival for the release of the restless dead; the Moon Festival, celebrating the harvest moon (September–October).

NOTES TO THE MAPS

1 POPULAR RELIGIONS

While the majority of the world's population (80 percent) claims some religious allegiance, what this means differs from state to state and even from faith to faith. In both Islam and Hinduism, the notion that religion is separate from life is unthinkable. In many states, Islam describes itself as a way of life rather than as a faith; and Hinduism as a term of reference to a 'faith' is something of an external creation. The name was introduced by the Persians to describe all beliefs in India – across the River Indus. Hindus themselves see what they believe as being how they live. There is no sense of one set of beliefs for everyday life and another for religious life. Judaism is also particular, since it is both a way of life and an ethnic identity – not always linked to religious belief or practice.

For many people, religious identity goes hand in hand with ethnic, social and cultural identity. Thus questions about how much a faith is practised are not really appropriate to, say, Indonesia, or large swathes of Africa, Latin America or even China. For most people, their faith is not a matter of conscious choice. They are born into a given set of values and beliefs. Unless some major trauma shakes them or they move right out of their own culture, the faith of their birth remains their faith throughout life. This pattern can be disturbed. Certain faiths and New Religious Movements are committed to conversion, and the arrival of missionaries may also change religious allegiance. This is clearly shown in the decline of traditional beliefs worldwide since 1450 (see **2. Arrivals**).

In Christianity, the notion of religion as separate from life is largely a Protestant north European/North American idea, but its impact has been immense. Because much academic study of religion has sprung from northern Europe and North America, the Protestant division into a public, secular world and a private, religious world has coloured how religion is understood. This in turn has led to a greater marginalization of religion from social life, and not just in those areas where the secular/religious division is a historic one. Modern India has tried to restrain or contain religion by using this model of a divide between the secular and religious. The secular constitution it adopted on independence was a direct legacy of rule by a colonial power, and this artificial divide may well be contributing to present tensions in India.

In those areas where religions are expanding fast – notably in the states which replaced the former USSR and in Africa – religious commitment often carries with it powerful social, political and ethnic identity. A change in religion is often also a social and political statement.

In northern Europe, Australia and New Zealand the situation is very different. While a majority claim allegiance to a faith, under 50 percent on average attend church on a regular basis (see inset, 'Empty Pews'). The USA, while to a great extent sharing what is seen as a common 'secular' culture with northern Europe, has developed a high level of church attendance amongst those professing a faith. However it would be a mistake to equate religious life with church attendance. The recent growth of interest in religious and spiritual issues in 'secular' cultures is testimony to a growing willingness to explore such areas, albeit not necessarily through conventional channels. Nevertheless, there is in these countries a continued steady growth in secularism – also often to be found in the educated urban classes outside Western Europe.

Empty pews highlight the gap between professed belief and practice, but TV and radio are another common means of worship throughout Europe. Church attendance in Norway, for example, has historically never been high due to the distances between places of worship and extremes of climate. But over 50 percent listen to the Sunday morning service on radio or TV. In Western Europe overall, however, the decline in weekly attendance at a place of worship does indicate a decline of religious observance.

Sources to the map:
Barrett, David B., *World Christian Encyclopedia*, Nairobi: Oxford University Press, 1982; Brierley, Peter, ed., *UK Christian Handbook 1992–3*, London: MARC Europe, 1992; Harris, Ian and others, eds., *Contemporary Religions*, Harlow: Longman, 1992; Harvey, Peter, *An Introduction to Buddhism*, Cambridge: Cambridge University Press, 1990; Horrie, Chris and Peter Chippindale, *What is Islam?*, London: Virgin, 1991; Shaikh, Farzana, ed., *Islam and Islamic Groups*, Harlow: Longman, 1992.

2 ARRIVALS

By 1450, Christianity appeared to be almost exclusively a white European religion, while Islam, with its heartlands in the Middle East, was primarily an Arab and Turkic religion. From the 1450s onwards, both Christianity and Islam began a new phase of expansion. Christianity, because of advances in navigation, moved out by boat to travel the world, starting with the voyages of Henry the Navigator. His Portuguese sailors crept their way round the northern coast of Africa, making the first new European landfall in West Africa in 1445. This landfall explains the early arrival of Christianity in Equatorial Guinea; and these early voyages opened the way for the major expeditions of the late 15th century.

In Islam, the fall of Constantinople in 1453 left the way clear for a sweep of the Ottoman Empire right across Eastern Europe to the gates of Vienna. Islam also experienced a revival in many traditional Muslim areas as a response to the increase in Christian missionary work which followed the explorers' ships. This in turn led to renewed Islamic mission especially in North Africa and India.

The development of Christianity was the more dramatic. By the newly-discovered trade routes across the seas, West European nations such as Spain, Portugal, England and the Netherlands, took both Christianity and colonialism around the world. The 'discovery' of the Americas was to have the greatest impact, but the spread of Christianity around the coastline of West, Southern and East Africa and into parts of Southeast Asia marked a major shift in the religious alignment of these large areas. By land, Russia was to colonize and Christianize Siberia from the 1600s onwards.

Following the capture of Constantinople in 1453, Islam spread into Europe yet more deeply. At one point in the 17th century, the Muslim Ottoman Empire controlled Greece, Bulgaria, Romania, Hungary and the area of former Yugoslavia. This proved to be a passing phase. More significant was its deeper penetration into North Africa and into Southeast Asia, consolidating and expanding its presence in both areas throughout the last four hundred years.

At that time most of the rest of the world, including the Americas, Australasia and the majority of Africa, practised local traditional religions, largely unaffected by any major world religion. Unlike Christianity or Islam, none of these cultures made universal claims for their teachings, nor did they experience the missionary drive which propelled Christianity and Islam across the world.

The expansion of Christianity and Islam rudely altered the world. Christianity, in particular, brought with it colonization and the impact of Western religion, diseases, and slavery reduced the numbers of indigenous peoples dramatically. In certain areas, indigenous faiths were literally wiped out. This, combined with major programmes for the conversion of indigenous peoples by both religions, has led to the virtual eclipse of indigenous religions in vast areas of the world. (For areas in which they have survived, see **9. Traditional Beliefs**.)

The rise of Marxism/Leninism and its associated secularism had a formidable impact on the practice of Buddhists, Christians, Jews and Muslims throughout the world. Communist states contributed more than any other cause to the persecution of faiths and loss of religious power. The collapse of Communism in the former USSR and Eastern Europe in 1991 has resulted in a remarkable revitalization. Religion is being rediscovered even where Communism is still powerful and asserting official disapproval, as in China and North Korea. Religious revival is not just an attempt to return to the past, for the faiths have all been changed by their experience. The survival of religious teachings, practices and beliefs where no outward sign is permissible (for example, Albania, 1967-91, or China during the Cultural Revolution, 1966-76) has taken many by surprise.

The dates given on the map indicate the first recorded arrival of a new faith, other than that which prevailed before 1450.

Sources to the map:
G. Barraclough, ed., *The Times Concise Atlas of World History*, London: HarperCollins, 1988; Barrett, David B., *Cosmos, Chaos and Gospel*, Birmingham, Alabama: New Hope, 1987; Barrett, David B., *World Christian Encyclopedia*, Nairobi: Oxford University Press, 1982; Shaikh, Farzana, ed., *Islam and Islamic Groups*, Harlow: Longman, 1992.

3 ROOTS AND BRANCHES

The roots of religious change and division are diverse. They do not necessarily stem from theology and may owe much to political, economic, and social issues.

When a faith moves across borders and cultures, it may have to adapt to new conditions. New forms may develop, different from or even at odds with more traditional interpretations. Buddhism, for example, spread from its original homeland in India, into China, Tibet and Japan. Many new schools of Buddhism arose that were not in conflict with earlier traditions, but made sense within the new cultures.

Political and ethnic differences may also create new schools, divisions or denominations. The success of the Protestant Reformation in 16th-century Europe owes as much to the rise of nationalism, expressed through the evolution of such 'national' churches as the Church of Sweden or the Church of England, as it does to substantial theological disagreement.

Some divisions have arisen from the desire of people to make a faith their own and from resistance to religious authority. Local expressions of an international faith may be allowed – even encouraged – as a source of vitality.

The key denominations, schools and groups within the major faiths are given below. There are myriad smaller ones including, for example, as many as 20,000 Christian denominations.

Buddhism. There are two major divisions, the Southern school, known as Theravada, and the Northern school, Mahayana. Theravada or 'Teaching of the Elders' is considered to be the oldest school and its holy books, the Pali Canon, the ones closest to the words of the historical Buddha. The Pali Canon has shaped Buddhism in Sri Lanka, Myanmar, Thailand and much of South-east Asia. Mahayana or 'Great Vehicle' arose around 2000 years ago and its teachings have shaped Buddhism throughout China, Korea, Japan, Tibet and Mongolia.

Christianity. There are three major divisions. The Roman Catholic Church and Orthodox Church, originally the eastern and western wings of the same Church, finally split into two sections in 1054. Differences over interpretation of authority and theology brought out tensions between the newer, Eastern Roman empire based on Constantinople and the older Western Roman empire based on Rome. The 16th-century Protestant revolution reacted against Roman Catholicism and created new denominations. Some, such as Lutherans and Anglicans, essentially continued the old style of Church with bishops and other Catholic practices, but made kings head of the Church, rather than the Pope. Over time, other Protestant denominations developed which rejected bishops and the Catholic theology of the state churches. Presbyterians, Congregationalists or Quakers all sought to develop models of leadership and theology which they believed were those practised by the early Church.

Hinduism. Hinduism is not really a single faith so it is not appropriate to suggest divisions. Hindus often refer to their faith as Sanatana Dharma or Eternal Truth, one of its ancient names. There continue to be hundreds of different ways that this is expressed, the two main forms being Vaishnavite (special devotion to Vishnu) and Shaivite (special devotion to Shiva).

Islam. In the mid-7th century CE, Islam divided, over the source of religious authority within the faith, into two major divisions, Sunni and Shi'a. The word Sunni derives from the Arabic 'code of behaviour', the body of traditional law that derives from the teachings and acts of the Prophet Muhammad. Sunni Muslims hold that the first three caliphs were all Muhammad's true successors and Sunnis form the majority of Muslims. They follow one of four main schools of law, Hanafi, Hanbali, Maliki or Shafi, all founded by Muslim jurists in the 8th and early 9th centuries.

The Shi'a believe that Ali was Muhammad's first true successor and the term Shi'a originally referred to the partisans (shi'a) of Ali. There are a number of major sub-groups, the largest being the Ithna'shaariyya (the Twelvers), so-called because they believe that the twelfth imam of the line of Ali was not murdered and did not die when he disappeared at 4 years old. They believe he will reappear as the al-Mahdi – the chosen one – who will herald the end of the world. The Zayids are a further sub-group. They were founded by the 5th imam after Ali and are now found primarily in the Yemen.

The Ibadiyah was the first group to split away from the main body of Islam, while claiming to preserve the true teachings of Islam. Based on a group around Khadijah, the Prophet Muhammad's wife and first convert to Islam, they are very strict in their observance and have little contact with other Muslim groups.

Judaism. Since the map shows only the divisions of majority religions, Jewish groups do not appear. Orthodox Jews, who are in the majority, assert the supreme authority of the Torah and believe that Jewish laws are not open to revision. Moves away from traditional or 'orthodox observance' have given rise to Reform, Liberal, Conservative, Reconstructionist and other forms of Judaism.

Sikhism. There is no major doctrinal division within Sikhism, but Sikhs are increasingly divided over whether or not there should be an independent Sikh political state – Khalistan – carved out of India and possibly part of Pakistan.

Taoism. The Taoism best known in the West is often called 'philosophical' Taoism after the great mystic writers Lao Tzu, Chuang Tzu and Lieh Tzu of the 5th to 3rd centuries BCE. However most Taoism as actually practised comes from what is called 'religious' Taoism founded by Chang Tao Ling in the 2nd century CE. Many different schools emerged over the next thousand years though only a few survive in any significant form today. Much of popular Chinese indigenous religion is Taoist-influenced, with a strong overtone of Chinese popular Buddhism.

In countries where there are different faiths or divisions, we have given details only for those forming the majority. The USA, for example, appears as majority Protestant, but within the Protestant majority, the Southern Baptists are the largest Protestant denomination, hence the symbol for Baptists.

Sources to the map:

Barrett, David B.,*World Christian Encyclopedia*, Nairobi: Oxford University Press, 1982; Harvey, Peter,*An Introduction to Buddhism*, Cambridge: Cambridge University Press, 1990; Horrie, Chris and Peter Chippindale,*What is Islam?*, London: Virgin, 1991; Shaikh, Farzana, ed., *Islam and Islamic Groups*, Harlow: Longman, 1992.

Acknowledgements:
Rupert Gethin.

4 CHRISTIANITY AND ISLAM

In the early 1990s, the two largest religions in the world are Christianity, with 1870 million adherents, and Islam, with 1014 million. Numerically, these are also the two fastest-growing faiths.

Christianity is growing across the world, especially in South Korea, Russia and sub-Saharan Africa. Islam is also growing worldwide, especially in the Muslim states of the former USSR. Both faiths are expanding largely through population increase: Christianity, in Europe (although in much of Western Europe populations are slowing down for other reasons), Russia, the Americas, Australasia and now in sub-Saharan Africa; Islam, in the Middle East, Central Asia, North Africa and Indonesia/Malaysia.

Both Christianity and Islam have explicit missionary teachings within their sacred books and within the tradition of the faith. While other faiths have an element of mission – usually seen as being carried out through personal contact and friendship – organizations within Christianity and Islam place a structural and financial emphasis upon taking their message to other peoples, as well as to non-practising members of their own faith (for the Christian missionary movement, see **14. The Mission**).

The two faiths are in most direct competition where sizeable populations still adhere to traditional beliefs. In Nigeria, Kenya or Tanzania, for example, the expansion of either Christianity or Islam is usually at the expense of local traditional religions, rather than each other.

While there are many small Christian communities in Muslim majority countries, often pre-dating Islam, their numbers are remaining static or decreasing through migration (as in Syria, Egypt or the Lebanon). However, there are large numbers of Filipinos, Korean and Christians from other countries, living and working across Muslim heartlands. There are also growing, active Muslim minorities in Western Europe. These communities, which began through links created by Western colonialism, have continued to expand through family connections or migrant labour from Muslim countries, and by acquiring converts from the host community.

Both faiths have found some cultures resistant. India and China, despite centuries of effort, have proved difficult for Christians to penetrate. In India, Christians are a tiny minority. In China, until very recently, never more than 1 percent of Chinese would call themselves Christian. For Islam, India has been a place of conquest and then retreat. In China, Islam has never reached beyond the Turkomanic and Mongolian tribes which it converted in the early centuries of Islam.

Sources to the map:

Barrett, David B.,*World Christian Encyclopedia,* Nairobi: Oxford University Press, 1982; Barrett, David B., and Todd M. Johnson, eds., *Our Globe and How to Reach It*, Birmingham, Alabama: New Hope, 1990; Brierley, Peter, ed., *UK Christian Handbook 1992–3*, London: MARC Europe, 1992; Harris, Ian and others, eds., *Contemporary Religions*, Harlow: Longman, 1992; Horrie, Chris and Peter Chippindale, *What is Islam?*, London: Virgin, 1991; Shaikh, Farzana, ed. *Islam and Islamic Groups*, Harlow: Longman, 1992; *Mainstream*, Journal of Christian Action for East-West Reconciliation, London, 1982.

Acknowledgements:
Mawil Izzi Dien.

5 HINDUISM

Hinduism is an all-embracing term to describe a vast array of beliefs, deities and traditions. Most Indians would not define themselves as Hindus. Indeed it could almost be said that religion in India is a complex web of indigenous beliefs. However there are certain key features of religious life which show a common root and understanding.

Most Hindus would accept a cyclical view of time, as being without origin and without destination. All is reincarnated, even the very gods themselves, and all is subject to change. Also most Hindus believe that the divine permeates everything, everything is divine and therefore mirrors or reflects the image of the divine. This captures the many ways of expressing belief in Sanatana Dharma – the Eternal Truth, and foundation of all life and reality. Hindus often refer to Vedic culture as being their own. This derives from the Vedas, the oldest Indian sacred books, and from which many of the essential tenets of Indian religious and social life derive.

There have been two significant phases of Hindu migration. From c.70 to 500 CE Hinduism was introduced to much of Southeast Asia and Indonesia along trade routes. Within Indonesia, it is the majority religion of Bali and is undergoing a revival on Java. The second phase began when Indians migrated to other parts of the British Empire, for example the Caribbean and Fiji, as indented labourers and for trade. Many of these communities have continued to grow through migration because of their strong links with specific areas of India. Most Hindu communities abroad co-exist peacefully, but occasionally, tension surfaces. In Uganda in 1972, 70,000 Asians were expelled by dictator Idi Amin. Many migrated to the UK.

The spread of Hindu ideas has been considerable throughout Europe, North America and Australasia. Hindu gurus have travelled west in response to the coming of Christian missionaries to India; and Westerners have been profoundly affected by visiting India and by translations of Hindu classics such as the Bhagavad Gita or the Upanishads. Hindu belief, imagery and philosophy offers a very different form of religious understanding from that practised in the West. It has created a wave of groups inspired by Hindu philosophy and practice – ranging from overtly religious movements such as the Ramakrishna Vedanta Mission to yoga and Hindu meditation. This has led to a revival of devotional Hinduism amongst many Hindus as well as attracting converts from other faiths and cultures.

The Jains are a distinct religious group whose founder Mahavira, broke away from the prevailing norms of Hinduism in the 5th century BCE. The Jains practise *ahimsa*, non-violence, and their religious orders of monks and nuns live in such a way as to minimalize harm to any living being. The most devout wear a gauze mask over their mouths to prevent them accidentally swallowing any insect, and they brush the path before them to remove ants and other insects. They believe that Mahavira was the last in a line of 24 *tirthankaras* (bridge-builders between this world and the spiritual world). The Jains have been a clearly identifiable community for over 2500 years.

Sources to the map:
Barrett, David B., *World Christian Encyclopedia* , Nairobi: Oxford University Press, 1982; Hinnells, J.R. ed., *A Handbook of Living Religions*, Harmondsworth: Penguin, 1984; Jackson, Robert, and Dermot Killingley, *Approaches to Hinduism*, London: John Murray, 1988; Williams, Raymond Brady, *Religion of Immigrants from India and Pakistan: New Threads in the American Tapestry*, Cambridge: Cambridge University Press, 1988.

Acknowledgements:
Ranchor Prime; Megan Rees.

6 BUDDHISM

Buddhism originated in north India, founded by Siddhartha Gotama, known as the Buddha – Enlightened One – in the 5th century BCE. For over a thousand years it flourished there, sending out teachers south and west to Sri Lanka, Myanmar, Thailand, Cambodia and Vietnam and north to Tibet, China and Japan. It then declined in India itself under the impact of Islam in the 10th to 12th centuries CE. Teaching that life is suffering and that attachment to suffering causes rebirth, Buddhism seeks to free the individual from the effects of suffering and ultimately from the effects of constant rebirth.

In the last 75 years, Buddhism has been subjected to more sustained persecution than at any previous time. Mongolia, a majority Buddhist country, became the second Communist state in the world in 1921. Communism took over China and then parts of Southeast Asia from the end of the Second World War until the 1970s. Thousands of monasteries were destroyed – Tibet lost virually all its monasteries - and most monks and nuns were forced out. In 1930 there were an estimated 738,200 monks and nuns in China; by 1986, there were only 28,000. In the early 1990s, Communism has lost some of its power and authority but still rules in China and elsewhere. However even where severe persecution persists, Buddhism is reviving.

Buddhism remains the religion of the majority in Thailand, Myanmar and Sri Lanka. It has recently become the majority religion again in Mongolia, as a result of new political freedoms. There are small pockets of Buddhists in Russia, in the republics of Buryat, Tuva and Kalmyk. They claim their Buddhist heritage from Mongolia. By the early 1990s Buddhism had gained strength in Indonesia, South Korea, Nepal, India, and China (though not in Tibet).

Buddhism is the state religion of Thailand and of Bhutan, a Himalayan kingdom which only recently opened itself to the outside world. There is likely to be a small Buddhist temple in most villages and in the rainy season the numbers of monks in Southeast Asian countries can double due to the number of young men taking temporary ordination. The Myanmar government is not anti-Buddhist, although increasing political and economic discontent has led to anti-government demonstrations and there is friction between monastic communities and the government.

In Japan, both Buddhism and Shintoism – the indigenous religion of Japan - are followed by the majority of people. Different temples are attended for different rites. Membership of Buddhist sects runs to 111 million. Due to traditional family affiliation many people claim membership of two or more sects, whether or not they are practising and it is impossible to gauge the actual number of practising Buddhists.

In India, the number of Buddhists has increased due to conversions, led originally by Dr B.R. Ambedkar, from the 'untouchable' castes (known as 'scheduled castes' since 1935). There has also been an influx of Buddhists fleeing from Chinese state oppression in Tibet. The spiritual leader of the Tibetans, the Dalai Lama, lives in exile in Dharamsala. While Buddhism is not under threat in most Indian states, Buddhists in Ladakh face mounting problems. Ties with Tibet have been cut off and the Muslim population is rapidly increasing. Buddhists in Bangladesh are also in difficulty, due to pressure from settlement by majority Muslim Bengalis and loss of their lands for hydro-electric schemes.

Over the last hundred years or so, Buddhism has spread throughout Europe, North America and Australia. Originally known only through translations of sacred texts and the commentaries of scholars and philosophers, since the 1960s Buddhist influence has increased as a result of great numbers of young people travelling to Buddhist countries. There is an increasing number of Buddhist centres and monasteries outside Asia, but it is virtually impossible to estimate the numbers of Westerners who practise Buddhism. Relatively few have joined organized religious orders. Many people find some aspect of Buddhist teaching, practice or belief helpful in their religious development, though they may not describe themselves as Buddhist.

Sources to the map:
Harris, Ian and others, eds., *Contemporary Religions*, Harlow: Longman, 1992; Harvey, Peter, *An Introduction to Buddhism*, Cambridge: Cambridge University Press, 1990; *International Buddhist Directory*, London: Wisdom Publicatons, 1985; Snelling, John, *The Buddhist Handbook*, London: Rider, 1987.

Acknowledgements:
Rupert Gethin; Mike Gilmore; Peter Harvey.

7 THE JEWISH DIASPORA

While numerically Jews have remained a small faith, the impact of their teachings, and in particular of the Hebrew Bible, on the world has been of greater significance than any other religious book. Both Christianity and Islam sprang from this Jewish understanding and scripture.

Most Jews today are to be found in either the USA or Israel. The state of Israel was created in 1948 – their first homeland for Jews since 70 CE when the Romans crushed a rebellion against their rule in Israel. For centuries before this, Jews had been living in scattered communities throughout the Middle East. After they were crushed by the Romans, Jews spread throughout the Roman Empire. Despite terrible persecutions and restrictions, Jews established significant communities in Spain and North Africa, Russia, Persia (modern Iran) and even India and China.

People of Jewish origin have varying degrees of personal commitment to Judaism or Israel. In fact, the numbers cited of Jews worldwide tend to vary because 'being a Jew' can have religious, ethnic or cultural meaning. In religious terms, a Jew is someone whose mother was Jewish and who lives by the Law of Moses and of the Torah – the Five Books of Moses or the first five books of the Bible. While many Jews with a Jewish mother would describe themselves as Jewish, they may well not be adherents of the faith.

The figures used in our cartogram reflect the 'core' Jewish population, namely those who clearly identify themselves as being religious Jews. This includes converts as well as those who have informally joined Jewish groups. It does not include those of Jewish descent who have no religion or follow another religion, those who were born Jewish but disclaim being Jewish, or non-Jewish members of Jewish households.

Over the last 200 years the location and size of the world's Jewish population has been radically altered: by mass migration from Europe and Russia in the late 19th to mid-20th century, mainly to the USA; by the tragedy of the Nazi Holocaust, 1939–45 (see **26. Never Again?**), which destroyed the Jewish cultures of Germany and Eastern Europe; and finally, by the creation of the state of Israel in 1948. The inset cartograms show that whereas in 1800 the vast majority of Jews lived in Europe and Russia, by the end of the 20th century the majority live in the USA or Israel.

Israel offers automatic right of entry and citizenship to any Jew from anywhere in the world. In the early 1990s, the collapse of Communism in Eastern Europe and the former USSR is allowing tens of thousands of Jews to journey to Israel (see inset map, 'The Olim') and is straining the resources of the small state.

While the Jewish population of Israel is increasing through births and immigration, elsewhere in the world the numbers are static or dropping, due to migration, marrying out and general assimilation. Thus the Jewish core population of the UK in 1977 was 336,000. By 1992, this had fallen to 301,000.

Sources to the map:
Singer, David, ed., *American Jewish Year Book*, Philadelphia, Pennsylvania: The Jewish Publication Society, 1992.

Acknowledgements:
Yitzrak Rabichiya; Marlena Schmool; Community Research Unit, Board of Deputies of British Jews; The Jewish Agency, Jerusalem.

8 SIKHISM

Sikhism arose from the teachings of Guru Nanak (1469–1539), who tried to fuse the best in Islamic and Hindu teachings and practice, combined with an intense personal revelation of the nature of God. As a result of religious persecution, the Sikhs established their own community and gained a degree of independence within Muslim-ruled India. Eventually Sikhs began to spread beyond India, especially to countries formerly part of the British Empire.

Worldwide, the number and size of Sikh communities is gradually increasing. To give a sense of the spread and relative strength of Sikhism around the world, we illustrate the number of gurdwaras. The gurdwara – or temple – is the focus of Sikh religious and community life. A community can range from a few families to a few hundred families. The presence of a gurdwara indicates a Sikh community large enough to support both it and its associated institutions.

Within India, Sikhs are migrating to the Punjab in increasing numbers. This is in response to rising levels of disturbance and tension between Sikhs and the Indian government. In turn, these are partly due to a growth of Hindu nationalism and to Sikh aspirations for their own separate state of Khalistan (Land of the Pure). In 1984, to crush the growing Sikh independence movement, Indian government troops stormed the holiest shrine of Sikhism, the Golden Temple of Amritsar.

In the early 1990s, the situation is calmer, but Sikh insurrectionists and Indian troops still clash regularly, and the political debate has riven the Sikh community. While militant Sikhs are working towards the creation of an independent state, others wish only for greater Sikh autonomy within India. Sikhs see themselves as the only major world religion without a state of their own – and many cite the creation of Israel as their model.

Sources to the map:
Cole, W. Owen, and Piara Singh Sambhi, *The Sikhs: Their Beliefs and Practices*, London: Routledge and Kegan Paul, 1978.

Acknowledgements:
W. Owen Cole.

9 TRADITIONAL BELIEFS

The terms 'traditional' and 'tribal' beliefs are here used to distinguish those cultures and belief systems which are not part of a major world religion. While they may often share certain key features – such as reverence for nature and worship or veneration of ancestors – they are not linked by adherence to any central tenets of faith. Frequently they have been part of the same geographical setting for many thousands of years and have used this setting to develop myth and ritual. It is estimated, for example, that Australian aborigine culture has existed in Australia for up to 40,000 years.

However, a few cultures have travelled. Many traditional beliefs are shaped by what is loosely called Shamanism. This is the belief that there are two worlds – a spiritual, real world, and the world of material existence. A Shaman possesses an ability to communicate with the spiritual world through trances. Shamanism is thought to have originated over 8000 years ago in Siberia and to have migrated with the movement of peoples over the landbridge linking Siberia and Alaska. Elements of Shamanism are to be found throughout the Americas.

In many parts of the world, traditional beliefs and cultures survive only in inaccessible or difficult terrain – the last refuge of peoples who formerly inhabited more accessible land but who have been pushed back by more aggressive settlers. In the Amazon basin this process is still going on (see below). In China, many of the 64 recognized minority peoples live in mountainous areas where they were driven by the spread of the Han Chinese over the last 3000 years.

Though traditional beliefs form the majority faith in few states, their influence is still widespread. In China, popular religion is observed in most villages and towns. This is a mixture of traditional beliefs focusing on ancestors, and on the intermingling of the spirit world and the physical world, overlaid with a veneer of Buddhism and Taoism. In Japan, Shintoism, unlike many traditional beliefs, has a written, rather than oral, sacred literature.

Shintoism is a separate faith from Japanese Buddhism, but the two co-exist and many people follow both religions. Shintoism, like most local traditional beliefs, has neither sought nor gained a following outside its own people.

It has been the spread of Christianity and Islam that has affected traditional beliefs most dramatically over the last 500 years, fundamentally affecting the religious practice of indigenous peoples from Siberia to Africa, from the Amazon to the Australian outback. In some places, whole belief systems and formerly numerous indigenous peoples have completely disappeared.

In some areas, people have continued to practise tribal traditions as well as Christianity or Islam, which have either been changed by traditional beliefs or learned to accommodate them. The Catholic Spiritists of Brazil, for example, while clearly Roman Catholics, have incorporated specific characteristics of cults of African origin.

In some African states where Christianity or Islam has become the majority religion, traditional beliefs have mingled with them to the point of producing quite idiosyncratic expressions of faith, usually confined to a single area. The growth of 'indigenous churches' highlights the fusion of certain core Christian ideas with key elements of traditional belief. The Church of the Initiates in Gabon, for example, combines ancestor worship with specific Christian teachings and symbolism. A few churches have become missionary in their own right (see **10. New Religious Movements**).

There has recently been an increased interest in traditional beliefs amongst some people in the West. This may sometimes be a romantic quest for a physical Garden of Eden or for the Noble Savage, but such interest is bringing the insights of traditional peoples into a wider circle of religious awareness.

There has also been a revival in traditional beliefs among indigenous peoples of Australia, Canada and the USA – not always welcomed by the state. In Australia, aboriginal peoples have campaigned vigorously for the protection and return of land sacred to them, such as Ayers Rock – known as 'Uluru'. While the governments of individual Australian states have agreed to some demands, others are a continuing source of conflict. In the USA and Canada, pride in traditional beliefs and culture has led to a revival of interest, not just amongst Native Americans, but in the wider community.

Traditional beliefs and ways of life are still under threat – in some cases, at greater risk than ever before. The native peoples of the Amazon are under severe threats from logging, mining, flooding and the encroachment of ranching and urban centres. In the Sudan, pressure from northern Muslims on traditional peoples such as the Dinka has led to rebellion and warfare, endangering survival of the Dinkas' traditional way of life. Worldwide, there appears little hope that the traditions, beliefs and close links with the land of indigenous communities will remain intact.

Sources to the map:

Barrett, David B., *World Christian Encyclopedia,* Nairobi: Oxford University Press, 1982; *Sacred Spaces*, Winnipeg, Canada: Canadian Coalition for Ecology, Ethics and Religion.

Acknowledgements:

Ben Burt, Museum of Mankind, London; Ranchor Prime; Franca Tranza; Minority Rights Group, London; Survival International, London.

10 NEW RELIGIOUS MOVEMENTS

The New Religious Movements illustrated on the map have come into being since the early 19th century, but the most notable growth has been a 20th-century phenomenon. While many movements may be local only – as with the New Religions of Indonesia or the indigenous churches of Nigeria – some have moved across the world and gained a visible presence far from their place of origin. They are in fact new missionary movements, and their spread into other parts of the world is causing some alarm in areas traditionally adhering to Christianity or Islam.

Every major religion has at some time been a new religious movement, splitting away from older traditions: as Buddhism did from Hinduism, Christianity from Judaism, Sikhism from Hinduism and Islam. What marks out today's major faiths from myriad other faiths over the centuries, is their ability to survive, adapt and flourish, by speaking to the human condition.

The increase in communications this century has widely disseminated religious ideas, beliefs and teachings, throughout the world, many previously unheard of. There are over a hundred translations of the Taoist classic Tao Te Ching, enabling it to be used as a basis for a whole range of religious thought and belief, often different from its traditional use in China. The Christian Bible now appears in over 2000 languages, leading to a host of varied interpretations, often diverging from the understanding of mainstream denominations.

In some areas, traditional religious culture has been undermined by secularism and by a collapse of belief in authority. A faith may have become stuck in a particular historical model which takes no account of changing social needs or awareness; or it may be failing to re-express itself in a way which speaks to people today. In some states, institutional religion is trying to reestablish itself in the chaos reigning after decades of repression under Communism. The old church/state relationship cannot and should not be recreated. Majority religions are having to work out their new status, while the people are exposed to differing religious claims. Russia, in particular, is witnessing a wide array of new religious groups at work within its borders, not all of them genuine.

Most New Religious Movements have their roots in a major world religion. The only other movements on our map, arise from the growth of psychology and psychoanalytical methods, sometimes fusing with insights and beliefs from the frontiers of science or even from science fiction itself. Erhard Seminar Training (EST) is an example of what are termed 'self-religions' – which seek to enhance human potential through various techniques derived from psychoanalysis. The Scientologists are one of the best known of these groups. They believe that the individual is trapped by 'engrams' – negative experiences in childhood or even in the womb, which cripple and hold people back from full development. Using a system called 'Dianetics' founded by the former science fiction writer L. Ron Hubbard, they claim to be able to free the individual from these engrams and thus ensure a more fulfilled person.

New expressions of an existing faith may develop when it is transferred to a totally different culture. Buddhism, for example, was transformed as it travelled through China, producing new forms such as Chan (known as Zen in Japan) which have become part of the range of mainstream Buddhism. The opposite can happen. Ideas from another faith may be taken back home and developed within a different culture. The older religions have often disowned the activities of people who claim to be followers. The Unification Church of South Korea, for example, claims to be Christian and much of its language and symbolism comes from Christianity. Indeed, its full title is 'The Holy Spirit Association for the Unification of World Christianity'. But its leader, the Rev. Moon, believes he is the new messiah come to complete what Christ failed to achieve – the founding of a Perfect Family. Such dramatic divergence from mainstream Christian thinking means that Christianity rejects the Unification Church.

New Religious Movements often flourish in already pluralist and often volatile societies, though they rarely travel abroad. In Indonesia, over 60 million people follow indigenous New Religious Movements which are an officially recognized category of religion. In Vietnam, the Cao Dai faith and the Hoa Hao have over five million members between them.

Some New Religious Movements achieve a high public profile. They may set out to do so, like the Sanyasins of Osho (followers of Shree Rajneesh), who wear distinctive orange robes. More seriously, New Religious Movements may be accused of corruption or of abusing people through 'brainwashing' or totalitarianism. But most of them are neither sinisterly manipulative nor destructive. More often than not, they are targeted by parents or families who feel they have lost control of or contact with their children. Many more young people break off contact with their parents for reasons nothing to do with religion.

A few New Religious Movements may now be considered new religions per se. The Baha'is do not consider themselves to be a sub-group of Islam, but a new religion. They arose from Persian Islam (modern Iran) in the mid-19th century and by the end of the century had spread well beyond the Islamic world, often being embraced by those who wanted a faith similar to but not connected with Christianity. By contrast, the Ahmadiyas do consider themselves to be true Muslims, though they were rejected forcefully by mainstream Islam.

Most New Religious Movements are not the cranks and crazies of the Western popular press. They are usually serious, legitimate and highly-organized expressions of religious belief, or reworkings of older religious traditions. Many do not see themselves as having diverged from the main tradition, and often see themselves as more faithful to the original founder than the dominant expression of that faith.

Sources to the map:
Barrett, David B., *World Christian Encyclopedia*, Nairobi: Oxford University Press, 1982; Brockway, A.R., and J.P. Arjashkar, eds., *New Religious Movements and the Churches*, Geneva: WCC Publications, 1987.

Acknowledgements:
Eileen Barker; Charlotte Hardman; Ranchor Prime; The Baha'i International Community, Haifa; INFORM, London School of Economics.

11 UNITED DIVERSITY

The USA has developed prolific religious traditions and is sometimes described as offering a supermarket of religions. There are more expressions of 'Eastern' religions and New Religious Movements in the USA than anywhere else in the world – the highest concentration being probably in California. However, the vast majority of the US population professes allegiance to Christianity. With over 2500 different Christian denominations, the USA has the most diverse Christian scene in the world, though many of these denominations have one or two congregations.

Though the Protestant churches combined account for over half the US population, the largest Christian denomination is the Roman Catholics, at 30 percent. Of Protestants, the largest denomination is the Southern Baptist Convention with 14.9 million baptized members. The term 'Southern Baptist' arose when US Baptists split from the main church in 1845. Any slave owner was banned from being appointed a missionary and the Southern Baptists held a convention to oppose this ruling. In the 20th century, opposition to black civil rights has also been high in churches affiliated to the Convention, still known for their more conservative stance – even though they may have liberal members, such as President Clinton. The Southern Baptists are now found throughout the USA and overseas, where they have more missionaries than any other US church.

While the majority of Christians belong to the main denominations, their membership is declining. Roman Catholics, Southern Baptists and the Assemblies of God are holding on to their members or are increasing slowly; but Methodists, Presbyterians, Episcopalians, Disciples of Christ, United Church of Christ, Evangelical Lutherans and the Lutheran Missouri Synod, have all been declining markedly for decades. The number of Christians who attend church is much higher in the USA than other Western countries, but the dramatic growth is in those attending smaller, more local or fundamentalist/evangelical churches. Some 80,000 independent charismatic congregations have sprung up across the USA since 1980.

The TV evangelists have achieved a high profile – more for their off-station activities, such as mismanagement of finance and sexual behaviour, than for their programmes. Viewing numbers have declined in recent years and the effect of these tv stations on the religious life of the USA is small compared with their visibility.

Sources to the map:
Barrett, David B., *World Christian Encyclopedia*, Nairobi: Oxford University Press, 1982; Draper, Edythe, ed., *The Almanac of the Christian World, 1993–4*, Wheaton, Illinois: Tyndale House, 1992.

Acknowledgement:
John N. Vaughan.

12 FAITH IN THE FEMININE

The issue of patriarchy and matriarchy in world religions is a source of much heated debate within the religions themselves. All the world religions are in essence culturally patriarchal, though not necessarily so in their structural understanding of God or divine power. The founders of world religions were exclusively male (see **32. Foundations**) and their leaders are still usually male (see **29. Equal Rites**). But female figures, though not always as powerful as male figures, still have a strong presence within Christianity, Buddhism and Hinduism, if not within Islam or Judaism.

The argument rages as to whether this patriarchal dominance of religion is inherent to religion (as argued by Mary Daly and Daphne Hampson), or whether there has been a hijacking of the religious world by men (as argued by US theologian Elisabeth Schussler Fiorenza and archaeologist Marija Gimbutas). Some emphasize that there was once a predominance of matriarchal religions before the rise of the major religions over the last three thousand years. Others (such as feminist Riane Eisler) point out that many world religions originally showed much greater equality between men and women, and argue that this is reflected in earlier deities and practices. This important debate, on whether the nature of differences between the sexes in authority and power is a reflection of divine planning or a construct of humanity at certain stages of evolution, has gone on since the end of the 19th century, but only seriously sustained over the last thirty years.

Feminine deities and religious figures are clearly symbolic. Is the Virgin Mary, the earthly mother of Jesus, whom Christians believe to have been himself divine, the archetype of the dutiful mother the Mother of God, or does she take on a divine status of her own in popular religious culture? The Roman Catholic Church encourages devotion to the Virgin Mary and sightings worldwide are scrutinized by the Vatican, to minimize the influence of false claims, or claims not consistent with Roman Catholic understanding of the Virgin. Within recent years, there have been thousands of reported sightings, though few have been authenticated or proved to be of lasting significance. The Virgin often appears in places of great social and political tension.

The Chinese Buddhist deity, Kuan Yin, is the goddess of compassion and a fervent intercessor for those suffering on earth. In Hinduism, Kali may be fearfully displayed as the goddess of destruction, the consort of Shiva. She is revered as both the giver and destroyer of life. The Tibetan deity Tara is represented in 21 different forms and in her white or green forms she symbolizes compassion, the easing of human suffering and guidance to wisdom and salvation. It is largely in this role that she is popular in the Tibet and Himalayan region. In her more menacing red, yellow or blue forms she is fearful and awe-inspiring.

Such female figures undoubtedly have a powerful impact. For some critics, these images of the mother, of the compassionate or even of the fearful, are male creations representing male wishes or fears about women. For others, the notion of the feminine divine has subversive elements and represents an awareness of either an older set of beliefs about the goddess, or a subcurrent running through history which has always seen the divine as both male and female. For yet a third group, the debate about the maleness or femaleness of God is misplaced – any such description of God is inadequate since God is experienced through faith.

Sources to the map:

Baring, A., and J. Cashford, *The Myth of the Goddess*, London: Viking Arcana, 1991; Carroll, Michael P., *The Cult of the Virgin Mary*, Princeton, New Jersey: Princeton University Press, 1992; Foy, Felician A. (O.F.M.), ed., *The Catholic Almanac 1993*, Huntington, Indiana: Our Sunday Visitor, 1992; Naquin, B.S., and Chun-sang Yu, eds., *Pilgrimages and Sacred Sites in China*, Berkeley, California: University of California Press, 1992; Snelling, John, *The Buddhist Handbook*, London: Rider, 1987.

Acknowledgements:
Caroline Davis; Celia Deane-Drummond; Sandra Palmer.

13 DOUBTS AND CERTAINTIES

The issue of religion can be very difficult for some people. Some are uncertain that they can believe anything specific about God or the divine and thus classify themselves as agnostics. Others define themselves as atheists, and reject all belief in God or the divine. It is not socially acceptable everywhere to profess to being an agnostic or atheist. In a handful of states, such as Iran, it is even dangerous.

In many European states, belonging to a religion no longer carries with it the notion of full adherence to a set of teachings and there exists a form of agnostic Christianity. Many people, and not just in Europe, would wish to retain moral and ethical insights and codes of faith but abandon overt religious practices. They see themselves as personally agnostic but accept the need for society to adhere to a shared moral code. When adults in the UK have been questioned about religious education, over 50 percent regarded it as important for imparting a moral code, but not so important for imparting religious faith or truths.

Those who identify themselves as atheists often do so in order to make a stance, not just against the beliefs of any given religion, but against the whole apparatus of organized religion. They may take a position that religion is not rational or subject to reasoned study and analysis, and this may be fused with personal experience of the failings of religion. Some atheists regard religious faith as being a primitive state of mind, one which hinders the fullest development of humanity. Atheism can itself become a belief system, replacing God as the centre or purpose of life with humanity or the wellbeing of the planet. Atheists have been instrumental in founding many international humanitarian agencies such as the United Nations or the International Union for Conservation of Nature and Natural Resources.

The activities of official atheist states, former or otherwise, has caused problems for many atheists. Their suppression or eradication of religion has meant that as a movement rather than a personal stance the term 'atheist' is often regarded with suspicion.

Atheism continues to be the official position of the governments of China, North Korea and Cuba. Here, large organizations are to be found and impressive numbers are cited. It may be politically correct to be atheist in Communist countries, but judging by the collapse of such groups and in numbers of atheists once Communism falls, the conviction may not always run deep. China is an interesting example. While officially atheist and while religious oppression is still widespread, religion in China is experiencing revival in many different forms. This could be linked to the current climate of economic change. In Cuba and North Korea however, systems have remained largely unchanged for many years, and no such revival is evident.

In former Communist states like Hungary or eastern Germany, official atheism may no longer be as powerful but much higher numbers still claim to be agnostic than in Western Europe. The impact of atheism on religious belief has been considerable, especially in states with a Protestant background. It has weakened links with formal religion, legitimated dissent from religious values and traditions, and furthered secularization faster than anywhere in Western Europe with the exception of the Netherlands. Orthodox and Roman Catholic states would appear to have a stronger hold upon people even after 70 years of Communist rule.

The proportion of people who call themselves humanists and who belong to humanist organizations is small, although a few states – the Netherlands with 25 percent and Norway with 20 percent – are obvious exceptions. The nature of these groups varies from state to state. In some countries, they have a strong scientific basis and seek to confront what they see as the illogicality of religion. In others they have a quasi-religious foundation – arising from attempts to provide a human-centred faith in the late 19th century. The American Ethical Union is one of the most clear examples. Yet others arise primarily from a concern for human wellbeing, with an emphasis on the need for moral and ethical codes based on human interests and values and not shaped by reference to a divine will or purpose. The Humanistisch Verbond Belgie (Belgian Humanist League) is an example of this.

There are many who would count themselves as agnostic, or as having no particular faith, and the number is growing. But the numbers of atheists and humanists worldwide are not sizeable and are rarely growing rapidly, except perhaps in the Netherlands, France and Norway. Beyond this, there is no doubt that the legitimation of doubt and the quest for common human values, unrelated to specific religious teachings, has had a considerable impact even on those who profess a faith.

Sources to the map:
Barrett, David B., *World Christian Encyclopedia*, Nairobi: Oxford University Press, 1982.

Acknowledgements:
Matt Cherry; Rob Tielman; British Humanist Association, London; International Humanist and Ethical Union.

14 THE MISSION

The Christian missionary movement is as strong if not stronger than it has ever been. It has 4000 missionary organizations, over 308,000 full-time career missionaries and an annual expenditure of US $9.6 billion. It is far removed from the 19th-century stereotype of the missionary, dressed in white and paddling up the Limpopo, or the notion of going to a 'heathen' country to bring about conversions.

Christianity has always been a missionary religion – the Apostle Paul was its first major missionary figure. But in the 1990s, just 1 percent of all Christian missionaries go to countries with another majority religion. Almost all go to Christian majority countries in response to requests from local churches, a principal known as 'partnership'. A massive amount of time, energy and finance is spent on 'home' mission – mission within one's own country. This is not shown on the map. Further, the total impact of foreign mission is difficult to calculate since large numbers of Christians work abroad for non-Christian organizations and engage in part-time mission. Others go out under the auspices of groups not officially described as a missionary organizations.

As well as preaching and teaching, foreign missionaries today work on agricultural schemes, housing projects, schools, hospitals, counselling programmes, computer materials, information systems, church organizing. Most missionaries work within a major denomination; or as itinerant or independent evangelists. Some use TV or radio to spread the gospel, some still travel on foot, by camel or by bicycle.

The largest numbers of missionaries still come from the traditional mission-sending countries of Western Europe and the USA. But increasingly, former 'mission field' countries are sending sizeable numbers to work abroad – sometimes back to the old, mission-sending countries themselves.

Since the collapse of Communism there has been a dramatic increase in foreign missionary activity in the new states of the former USSR and in Eastern Europe. There are over 300 US missionary groups now active in Russia. Many work with the established churches – Orthodox, Roman Catholic, Protestant and Independent but some missionary groups do not view Orthodox Christians or Roman Catholics as 'true' Christians, and have caused widespread dissent and anger. The Russian Churches are concerned that some missionaries view Russia as a blank sheet non-Christian country.

Protestant missionaries are 'invading' other areas where Orthodox or Roman Catholics have traditionally been in the majority, for example, in Central and northern Latin America. They are 'converting' Roman Catholics to the Protestant expression of Christianity – fundamentally altering the religious, social and political balance (see **31. Faith in the Future**).

Sources to the map:
AD 2000, Global Monitor, monthly newsletter, Birmingham, Alabama: New Hope; Barrett, David B., and Todd M. Johnson, eds., *Our Globe and How to Reach It*, Birmingham, Alabama: New Hope, 1990.

Acknowledgments:
Joseph Brankin; Conference for World Mission; National Missionary Council for England and Wales.

15 A WORLDWIDE CHURCH

The Holy Catholic Apostolic and Roman Church (or the Catholic Church) is the largest single group within a major world religion. Centred on the Vatican, a self-governing city state in Rome, it claims the allegiance of 1017 million believers, and is served by 1.5 million full-time professionals (priests, nuns, monks and lay leaders). It is the only religious group with full diplomatic representation to national governments as well as to international bodies such as the UN. 141 countries have ambassadors to the Vatican, including, most recently, Kirghizia, Mongolia and Romania. Indeed the Vatican is the oldest uninterrupted diplomatic service in the world.

There is currently an overall shortage of priests to administer to the faithful. Indeed there are some traditionally staunch Roman Catholic areas, such as most of South and Central America, where the number of priests per head of population is very low. Priests tend to be reserved for 'frontier' areas, such as India or Canada, or where finance is available, such as the UK or Belgium.

John Paul II, the current Pope and head of the Catholic Church, is the 263rd successor to St Peter, the first bishop of Rome. He is the first Polish Pope in the history of the Church. Through his extensive world travels, he has had more contact with the faithful than any previous Pope. His journeys were initially undertaken to restore confidence following uncertainty and change caused by the Second Vatican Council 1962–65. Through Vatican II, the Church reorganized, and frequently liberalized, its teachings and organization. But the present Pope has resisted much of the liberalization which followed Vatican II. In his visits abroad he stresses traditional teachings, such as the ban on artificial contraception.

The 4000 employees of the Vatican, including 1000 who live in the city state, are the centre of an enormous worldwide publishing, TV and bureaucratic network. A range of specialist Congregations and Councils, comprising Vatican staff and bishops from around the world, preserve the unity of the church's teachings. The Congregation for the Doctrine of the Faith is responsible for official statements of Roman Catholic belief. Since Vatican II there has been increased emphasis on the role of the laity in local decision-making.

Local authority is exercised through the bishops of 2355 dioceses across the world. Bishops gather on a national or regional basis to decide local policies. They visit the Vatican every five years to report to the Pope. A few senior bishops are nominated to the College of Cardinals. In the early 1990s there are 155 Cardinals whose location indicate power within the Catholic Church. For example, Italy has 37 cardinals, the most in the world. The USA has 11, France 9, Brazil 7, Spain 6, Germany 5 and Argentina, Canada, India and Poland, 4 each. Some are permanently based at the Vatican, as for instance is Cardinal Etchegaray of France, who heads the Pontifical Council for Justice and Peace. The College of Cardinals is responsible for the appointment, not necessarily from amongst their own number, of a new Pope on the death of the incumbent.

Sources to the map:
Annuario Pontificio, Rome: The Vatican, 1992; Foy, Felician A. (F.O.M.) *The Catholic Almanac 1993*, Huntington, Indiana: Our Sunday Visitor, 1992; *Statistical Yearbook of the Catholic Church*, Rome: The Vatican, 1993.

Acknowledgement:
Catholic Media Office, London.

16 ON AIR

Religious broadcasting is rapidly growing within many world religions. Broadcasting transcends national boundaries and has special appeal for certain religions as a means of sending their message worldwide.

The Christians control more airwaves than any other religion. This reflects partly the traditional emphasis on 'the word' and partly the wealth of many Christian majority countries. It is enhanced by the universal role of the English language. Christian broadcasts reach every single country in the world and have 1.6 billion listeners. They are transmitted by Christian-owned and operated stations (the UK has a handful, Brazil has 1300, and the USA over a thousand) or by state-operated facilities such as the BBC World Service. The secular media may also be quite open to supporting religious broadcasting. In the UK, the BBC supports regular religious broadcasting at no charge, as do independent TV channels.

While there are scores of Protestant international radio stations, such as AWR Radio in Costa Rica, Guam, Italy and Russia, or Christus Lebt in Germany, the single Roman Catholic station, Radio Vatican, is powerful enough to reach the whole world. Sixty countries have international transmitting stations belonging to Christian organizations. Many broadcast to a region, such as the Caribbean Radio Lighthouse in Antigua or the Central American Mission in Guatemala City. International groups include Trans World Radio, which covers the world by broadcasting from Albania, Cyprus, Netherlands Antilles, Sri Lanka and Swaziland.

Some governments try to block Christian broadcasts, but cannot do so effectively. However, 32 states at least nominally ban all internal broadcasting of the Christian message.

Sources to the map:
Barrett, David B., *World Christian Encyclopedia*, Nairobi: Oxford University Press, 1982; Barrett, David B., and Todd M. Johnson, eds., *Our Globe and How to Reach It*, Birmingham, Alabama: New Hope, 1990.

17 CHRISTIAN GIVING

While never a formal part of Christian teaching, the notion of giving some regular amount of personal income to the church, if only for a favoured charity, is to be found in all branches of Christianity. There has also arisen a tradition of giving aid for overseas development, partly as a result of the 19th-century missionary movement, partly because of continuing ties between the churches of the post-colonial world.

Most mainstream Christian churches in the West are now able to use formal ecumenical church channels for overseas aid – one of the real successes of the Ecumenical Movement (see **27. The Ecumenical Movement**). Protestant churches work through the development arms of the World Council of Churches and agencies set up by national churches – such as Christian Aid in the UK. Roman Catholic churches are highly organized with central fundraising programmes in 128 countries linked through the Vatican-based Caritas International.

In some countries, funds are allocated not just from personal donations from individual Christians or local churches, but from a church tax levied by the government. In Germany and Sweden in particular, Church aid agencies benefit from these taxes (see **23. God and Mammon**). Other charities rely mainly or entirely on direct donations.

The way aid is given differs. The agencies represented on the map are typical of the broad range of mainstream aid agencies. They usually choose projects and channel funding through local churches abroad.

The agencies do not fund Christian groups alone. Most have funding criteria which forbids consideration on the basis of religious affiliation. This being said, some aid agencies, big and small, especially from conservative Protestant churches, were created specifically to fund primarily Christian groups. Such groups tend to have a stronger link between aid and evangelization.

Christian aid agencies tend to favour projects which enable recipients to achieve self-reliance – through education, practical projects and the establishment of small scale industries and welfare. While the largest Christian agencies also respond to major emergencies such as floods or famines, their efforts are mainly directed to long-term solutions of global poverty, as can be seen in the pie-chart on Brot für die Welt, rather than on short-term emergency aid.

Sources to the map:
Agency yearbooks, annual reports and financial statements, 1991.

Acknowledgments:
Joseph Brankin; Derrick Knight; Barbara Stephens.

18 MUSLIM GIVING

The Five Pillars of Islam require Muslims to give or pay 'zakat', an obligatory tax on income, once a year. Zakat is leveled at a 2.5 percent minimum of personal capital wealth, after all basic necessities have been met. 'Basic necessities' are usually defined as being able to feed, clothe, house and educate those within the family. There is no legal force or administration which oversees the giving of zakat, which is left to personal honesty. It is often supplemented by further personal acts of charity. Both are given through the local mosque and are distributed locally or further afield through informal networks between mosques and Islamic organizations. A vast amount of Islamic aid is therefore untraceable or unrecorded in any accessible way.

During the 1980s, in part in response to similar Christian programmes, Muslim groups have begun to organize formal Islamic aid agencies, especially in the West where the informal networks are less strong. Aid is primarily given to Muslim states or to Muslim groups in non-Muslim states. Funds are given to develop local skills and projects such as cooperative businesses in areas of high unemployment or farming in areas of devastation. They are also given for emergencies – for example to Muslim refugees who may be fleeing from war or famine in such countries as Bosnia-Herzegovina, Somalia and the Sudan.

Only certain large agencies are shown on the map. Most Muslims still prefer to give through their own mosques and total Muslim aid channelled through Islamic agencies is, so far, not very large.

Most of the new agencies are based in the UK, although one of the largest is based in Pakistan. Its founder, Abdul Sattar Edhi, began by setting up free dispensaries in Karachi in the late 1940s, going on to develop and head a remarkable worldwide humanitarian agency.

Another form of aid, however, is given by Islamic states directly, in particular, Saudi Arabia. In this way, large sums are invested in development projects, usually in the poorer Islamic states or Islamic communities in countries such as Tanzania or Kenya. Such funds tend to be administered by Muslim religious missionaries and are usually for education, health and welfare programmes.

Sources to the map:
Agency annual reports and financial statements, 1990–1992; *Q News Magazine*, London.

Acknowledgement:
Iftikhar Awan.

19 INTEREST IN MONEY

Traditional Islamic economics was dominated by an injunction in the Qur'an not to charge interest on loans of money. Through interaction with Western banking systems, however, interest charges have found their way into Islamic life. Within some Islamic states and amongst certain Muslim groups there has developed a campaign to renew Islam and the creation of a non-interest based financial system is a central plank of their programme.

Qadi Abu Bakr, a 12th-century Muslim teacher, describes usury as 'any unjust increment between the value of the goods given and the value of the goods received'. Muslims say that true trade is based on justice, that is, the exchange of equal for equal. Usurious trade is based on injustice, that is asking for more and giving less or nothing in return. Islam is not against the making of profit, but according to Islamic law, this profit can only be gained justly if the person who invests risks both success and failure. The basis of the argument against interest is that the investor takes virtually no risk and does not contribute to the exchange.

Early Judaism and Christianity also banned the charging of interest, or usury. Judaism was forced to relinquish this stand because of the precarious existence of Jews within first the Roman empire and later within various Christian countries and empires. The Christian church forbade usury during the Middle Ages. In the mid-16th century, however, Protestant Calvinist reformers gave usury official approval.

Many Muslims point out that according to the Qur'an, usury is against the Will of God. Since the Muslim world has been increasingly drawn into modern, Western banking, there have been attempts, in a number of Islamic states, to establish trading and banking facilities along Islamic principles. Such banks are trying to operate on a national level and to control other forms of banking. Some Muslim banks seek the compromise of a mixed system and provide facilities for 'normal' as well as non-usury banking.

The notion of non-interest banking is in itself difficult; it is also difficult to challenge the might of the Western banking system. Even Muslim opposition is quite widespread, on the grounds that older, pre-capitalist models of trade as found in the Qur'an are no longer appropriate to today's world. Nevertheless, attempts to develop non-usury trading are gaining popularity. Muslims keen to return to Islamic values use the debt crisis that beset many Latin American, African and Asian countries during the 1980s, as an example of the destructive impact of interest-charging banking.

Sources to the map:
Bank reports; *New Horizon*, London: Institute of Islamic Banking and Insurance, 1992.

Acknowledgements:
Iftikhar Awan; Fazlun Khalid; Swahela Siddiqui; International Association for Islamic Banks, London.

20 STATE FAIR – AND UNFAIR

State neutrality on religion, or religious tolerance, is undoubtedly gaining in worldwide support. In the West, the secularization of elites, a general increase in individualism and personal choice, and the decline in the significance of public religious practices, mean that religion is more and more seen as a matter of personal choice – of little concern to the state unless specific religious activities challenge its interests.

Both Sweden and the UK have formal state religions, yet over this century the degree of control exercised has markedly declined and a *de facto* division allowed or even encouraged. In Iceland, which has Lutheranism as the state religion, the state also recognizes and funds all other religions in the country, including the Norse religion, Asa.

The links between a religion and national identity are rooted in the past and built up over centuries. In states without a religious history, or where the state itself has been subject to change, the ties with religion are more tenuous. The map shows clearly that few 'new' nations – especially post-colonial states – have formal ties with any one religion. Where they do, such ties are usually with a pre-colonial faith, as in Pakistan or Myanmar. For the majority of 'new' African states, the concept of mature statehood assumes that religious practice is a matter of individual choice, so long as it does not endanger others or state interests.

Yet in many countries of the world, the concepts of state and religion are still intimately intertwined. In many Muslim countries, it is inconceivable that the head of state should not be a Muslim, or that the government should not follow Islamic law or attempt to rule according to Islamic principles. This stems from Islam's belief that the Qur'an and Shari'ah contain all that is necessary for the proper governing of a state.

The state may exert its authority, over religions and also its people, through either recognition or oppression. The state may also seek to protect the dogmas and certainties of its ruling group and elite. Much of the conflict between Marxist-Leninist regimes and religious communities comes from the fact that Marxism-Leninism was to all intents and purposes a belief system itself – and particularly threatened by other belief systems.

A few countries, having experienced religious conflict, seek to hold the religions in balance. Belgium, for example, recognizes five religions, and Indonesia recognizes five religious groups.

In a number of states during the 20th century, political revolutions have broken once close ties with a majority faith: between Russia and the Orthodox Church, for example, and Cambodia and Theravada Buddhism. This radical change often instigated a period of persecution, for both the majority religion and other religions too. From 1967–91, Albania, the most draconian of all Marxist-Leninist states, outlawed all religious practice.

Sources to the map:

Barrett, David B., *World Christian Encyclopedia* , Nairobi: Oxford University Press, 1982; Harvey, Peter, *An Introduction to Buddhism*, Cambridge: Cambridge University Press, 1990; Horrie, Chris and Peter Chippindale, *What is Islam?*, London: Virgin, 1991; Shaikh, Farzana, ed., *Islam and Islamic Groups*, Harlow: Longman, 1992; Szajkowski, Bogdan, ed., *New Political Parties of Eastern Europe and the Soviet Union*, Harlow: Longman, 1992.

Acknowledgement:
Mawil Izzidien.

21 LIFE AND SOUL OF THE PARTY

The relationship between religions and political parties may range from a low-key historical link with emotive connotations (as with certain Christian Democrat parties in Western Europe) to the existence of clear religious/political goals (as with the Bharatiya Janata Party, or BJP, the Hindu nationalist party of India).

The desire to separate religion and politics is largely European, arising from the need to end the long religious wars of the 16th and 17th centuries and from the growing separation of religion as an individual, private experience away from the public, secular world. This makes little sense to many people elsewhere, especially in those states where the popular faith is totally integrated with the way of life.

Most political parties with an overt religious tie (when the name of the religion, for example, is part of the name of the party) can turn to members of their affiliated faith for financial or practical assistance at elections or during a referendum. The name of a religion within the party name may also act at a subliminal level – especially among minority communities such as other religious or ethnic groups. It explains, perhaps, why German and Dutch Christian Democrat parties in Europe have chosen to maintain the term 'Christian'. In some states, such as the UK (excluding Northern Ireland) the notion of formal religious affiliations for political parties is simply unthinkable – especially as the UK becomes a more and more pluralist society.

In some countries, Catholic Italy and Spain in particular, there has been a long tradition of religious parties or parties with religious links. In Italy, the Christian Democratic Party was the main opposition to the Communist Party and in Spain, Franco relied on the Church to support him against the left. In others, the links between religion and party represent an ethnic or ideological association. In the newly-emerging democracies of central Europe, such as Hungary, the use of the term 'Christian' has anti-Communist and nationalist connotations. However, in protest against the assumed link between Christianity and conservative politics there also developed a tradition of Christian socialism, which helped form a number of Labour Parties, as in the UK or Australia. However, these parties have never overtly claimed to be Christian.

In some Islamic states, overtly religious political parties may represent a backlash after decades of Communism, as in the emerging republics of Central Asia. They may also, as in Algeria where the Islamic Salvation Front (FIS) was eventually banned in 1992, be a response to a perceived weakening of traditional values because of Western influence.

In some states, religious parties are formed in support of a religious and/or ethnic minority. The Islamic parties in Bulgaria fall into this category. Others have been formed in response to longstanding religious/political tensions, such as the Catholic and Unionist (Protestant) parties in Northern Ireland.

In other states, especially certain Muslim majority states, it is simply inconceivable that a political party could be ideologically or structurally linked to anything other than the dominant faith of the country, especially where the self-understanding of that faith is that it contains within it a unique revelation of God's laws for the running of society.

The use of religion to assert moral high ground in politics is not confined to the political parties per se. In the USA there was no formal link in the 1980s between the Republican Party and the popular, conservative, Christian movement, the Moral Majority, but the influence of such Christian groups on government decisions was considerable.

Sources to the map:
Coggins, John and D.S. Lewis, eds., *Political Parties of America and the Caribbean*, Harlow: Longman, 1992; Derbyshire, J. Denis, and Ian Derbyshire, *World Political Systems*, Edinburgh: Chambers, 1991; Hutchinson Gallup, *Info 93*, Oxford: Helicon Publishing, 1992; Lewis, D.S. and D.J. Sagar, eds., *Political Parties of Asia and the Pacific*, Harlow: Longman, 1992; Szajkowski, Bogdan, ed., *New Political Parties of Eastern Europe and the Soviet Union*, Harlow: Longman, 1992.

Acknowledgements:
Lee Kenyon; James Palmer.

22 GENERATION TO GENERATION

Every education system in the world owes its origins to religious schools and the concern for education within the major faiths. Religions have always made education a high priority: to ensure continuity of the faith, to pass on stories and beliefs, and to maintain the moral and social wellbeing of the community. Thus, many of the world's greatest universities and centres of learning have religious foundations, such as Oxford and Cambridge in the UK, Harvard in the USA and Al-Azhar University in Cairo, Egypt. Over the last hundred years or so, states have generally set out to wrest control of education away from religion. In 19th-century Germany, for example, Bismarck's nationalist goals for unification were strongly objected to by the churches. In the UK, the state's policy of acquiring control of education was part of the growing secularization of national institutions.

In some countries, religious education is a state subject, taught by qualified teachers, trained largely by the state or in accordance with its requirements. In some states, as in Sweden, its purpose is to inform about the role of religion, as central to a mature understanding of culture and society. In others, it may be part of an agreement with the majority faith, to ensure that children become familiar with the faith of the culture (as in Bahrain, a Muslim majority state and the Dominican Republic where the majority of people are Roman Catholic). In the increasingly plural societies of Western Europe (the UK is a good case in point) religious education is being broadened to include teaching not just about the majority faith but other faiths as well.

In a few countries, religious education is not a formal part of the state curriculum, but religious teachers are allowed to hold special lessons on school premises, which pupils may opt to attend or not. In India, for example, religious education is optional at the choice of parents or children, and offered out of normal school hours. This is the case even in schools still under the authority of a church.

In others, religious education is not permitted within the school curriculum. In the USA this has been a historic position because of the separation of church and state in the US constitution. In the early 1990s it is beginning to change in certain states such as California. In China religious education is not permitted because the state is officially atheist.

In the new states of the former USSR and Eastern Europe, the role of religious education is under scrutiny, as is education in general. In the early 1990s it appears that state religious education will be introduced, and that many states will follow Western Europe in not limiting it to a single faith. In Poland, debate on the role of the Roman Catholic Church in the country as a whole has centred on the form of religious education to be taught in state schools.

In Western Europe syllabusus may include the study of faiths not represented within the population at large. However teaching of Christianity, the majority faith, may still predominate in some states. In the world in general there is a broadening going on within religious education and states are tending to move away from narrow and confessional-based syllabuses. Religious education is more and more judged by educational standards relating to child development, rather than by religious standards of conversion or of nurturing children into a specific faith.

Sources to the map:
Barrett, David B., *World Christian Encyclopedia,* Nairobi: Oxford University Press, 1982; *British Journal for Religious Education*, Christian Education Movement, Derby, UK.

Acknowledgements:
Alan Brown; Clifford Payne; National Society for Religious Education, London.

23 GOD AND MAMMON

One of the ways in which religion can be effectively monitored is through financial control by the state. At its most extreme, a country may give funding to cover the bulk of the costs of the majority faith's operations. In return, the faith acts as a branch of the state, usually benignly. The Turkish government, for example, in a policy instituted soon after Turkey became a secular republic in 1923, substantially contributes to the salaries of all imams in order to gain their political neutrality.

A few other states control funding almost totally. In both Saudi Arabia and Sweden for example, the state professes one single specific religion which then becomes closely involved in the process of government. In Saudi Arabia, the practice of Islam is enforceable by law and the imams are all state officials. In Sweden, a church tax is levied on all citizens regardless of religious persuasion and Lutheran clergy are paid by the state to record all births and deaths in their area.

In traditionally Catholic countries, such as Bolivia, the Church has been seen as the third pillar of society, alongside the military and the ruling class. This has been reflected in the finances made available for clergy and for religious functions. By the early 1990s, the status and funding of the Church in many South and Central American states is being reduced. This is because the Church increasingly identifies with the poor and dispossessed, because of the rise of Marxist-influenced sections within the Church – especially those engaged in liberation theology – and because of the Church's general call for greater human rights.

In a few countries, the state seeks to maintain a balance between different religious groups and thus relies on a policy of even-handedness. In this way it hopes to ensure that all major religions are indebted to it and that none is officially favoured. Indonesia has long undertaken a careful balancing act between five major religions or religious groupings and funds them all according to their numerical strength. In Iceland, all religions are eligible for state funding, including the Norse, pre-Christian faith, Asa.

Yet other states offer substantial funding to the major faith, but ask for no specific favours in return. Germany, for example, raises a church tax to fund both Roman Catholic and Protestant evangelical Lutheran churches. Although both are expected to provide religious education teachers and they act as major charities both in Germany and overseas, the state exerts little or no control over use of the money.

Most states give very little financial help to their faiths. They may not support religion on principle (as in the case of China, Cuba, the USA and France); or because of political differences with the majority faith (as in the case of Mexico and Uruguay); or because they are relatively new states without a history of religion and state being virtually one and the same (as in the case of Zambia, Chad or Australia: all relatively recent, secular states, with no formal links to religion).

Governments will usually provide some minimal support however: via tax relief, assistance for charitable work, education, or the maintenance of historic sites. China, for example, is restoring ancient temples (see **6. Buddhism** for the many destroyed during the Cultural Revolution 1966–76) but although some are allowed to be used for religious purposes, the government prefers to see them converted to museums.

Official state religions are not necessarily funded by the state. The Church of England is the state religion of England, but receives no state funding for its own activities, other than a little help with historic buildings and for civic roles including military chaplaincies. However, the UK government does give charitable status to most religions and thus exempts them from certain taxes.

Sources to the map:
Barrett, David B., *World Christian Encyclopedia*, Nairobi: Oxford University Press, 1982; Shaikh, Farzana, ed. *Islam and Islamic Groups*, Harlow: Longman, 1992; press reports.

Acknowledgement:
Josephine Edwards.

24 ISLAMIC LAW

Islamic law is founded upon the Qur'an, seen as the infallible word of God, and upon the Hadith, the sayings, actions and silent approval of the Prophet Muhammad. God is seen as the supreme lawgiver, and his laws are deemed to be for the whole of creation, not just for human beings. The formal term, Shari'ah, means the 'clear path', indicating correct ways of behaviour covering religious, political, social, domestic and even private life.

Throughout Muslim history, issues of interpretation have arisen, necessitating debate and discussion. In arriving at a legal decision, there has to be in theory a consensus of opinion by every scholar, but in practice it tends to be by majority consensus. This is called Ijma – literally 'agreeing upon'. Shari'ah is created by the Qur'an, the Hadith and Ijma.

There are four major schools of thought within the Shari'ah, and Sunni Muslims always belong to one of these: Maliki, Shafi, Hanafi or Hanbali. They are named after the 8th and 9th-century jurists who endeavoured to clarify and set down the law. According to Sunni law, the ruler of an Islamic state is free to choose the school of his choice, just as individuals have the right to be tried according to the school of their choice. The Hanbali school is the most strict and is not found outside Saudi Arabia, where it is the official state law.

Within Shi'a Islam, which does not follow any of these Sunni schools, the 'ulama' – or council of twelve Shi'a elders – is the central political and legal institution. The judges appointed by the ulama eventually became known as ayatollahs, and formed their own courts. In Iran, the ulama is the supreme governing body and the court of appeal for the faithful. The state enforces the Shari'ah law.

While Shari'ah is binding upon all Muslims, it is officially only binding upon non-Muslims when they live in Muslim countries, and even then, only according to a special format. In states which follow Shari'ah, for example, while alcohol is forbidden to Muslims under the Shari'ah, it is permissible for non-Muslims to drink alcohol in private, and in ways that will not cause offence to Muslims.

The application of Shari'ah by Muslim majority countries differs considerably. Certain states operate a purely secular system. Turkey, for example, has a legal system based on a secular Italian model, and Shari'ah has no legal validity. Others, often as a result of colonial influence, have a hybrid system which combines secular, Western legal interpretations and structures with elements of Shari'ah. In Morocco, for example, a mixed legal system was introduced in 1961, based partly on Maliki Shari'ah laws and partly on French civil codes. Indonesia, with one of the world's largest Muslim populations, has a system based upon a secular Dutch model, and Shari'ah is only applied in the religious courts, which deal with personal and family matters.

Yet others have Shari'ah as the total legal code for the country, and strictly enforce it. Iran employs the entire Shiite version of Shari'ah. In Pakistan, although secular lower courts exist, they are supervised by Shari'ah courts which have the power to overturn any 'non-Islamic' laws and judgements.

In countries where authority is invested in the monarch, such as Oman, the United Arab Emirates and Saudi Arabia, the monarch and the Shari'ah are the only source of law.

In a number of Muslim majority countries, the Shari'ah often acts as a focus for the call for Islamic renewal. In Egypt, the Muslim Brotherhood wishes to enforce Shari'ah as a means of reforming and renewing what it sees as a decadent society, tainted by secularism. Similar models are being voiced by radical groups in the Central Asian states of the former USSR, and in parts of north Africa, in particular Algeria. The imposition of strict Shari'ah in the Sudan has led to tensions both with Christians and tribal peoples in the south, but also with many Muslims in the north.

Sources to the map:
Horrie, Chris and Peter Chippindale, *What is Islam?* London: Virgin, 1991; Shaikh, Farzana, ed., *Islam and Islamic Groups*, Harlow: Longman, 1992.

Acknowledgement:
Mawil Izzi Dien.

25 RELIGION AT WAR

In virtually every one of the world's 480 major wars since 1700, each side has imagined itself to be exclusively on the side of God, Gott, Allah, Dieu or other names for the deity.

Religion is often so closely linked with ethnic or national identity as to be seen as inseparable from them. Thus a struggle for expressions of ethnic or national identity is experienced as a religious war. This is so of the current unrest in the Punjab, created by Sikh demands for a separate Sikh state.

Other wars are built upon a history of religious tension which now fuses with other social factors to produce violence. For example, the struggle between Armenia and Azerbaijan over the Armenian enclave of Nagorno-Karabakh in Azerbaijan is often described as a Muslim (Azerbaijan) versus Christian (Armenian) war.

Religion evokes powerful emotions and commitments. It is capable of producing believers whose faith moves them to acts of great self-sacrifice and charity. At the same time it can produce believers who feel that their faith calls them to struggle violently in what they believe to be a just cause. A recent example is the Hindu/Muslim tension in India most recently focused on Ayodhya. Here, a mosque built in the 15th century was destroyed in 1992 by militant Hindus because it is believed to have been built over the birthplace of the Hindu god Rama. While the majority of Hindus and Muslims have lived together peacefully for generations, extremists on both sides are capable of arousing violence through use of powerful religious symbols.

In many faiths, the issue of whether warfare is permissible has given rise to various theories of the just war. Such theories seek to define whether believers can ever engage in the use of violence. The usual conclusion is that violence – including warfare – is only acceptable in pursuit of a greater good. The problem, however, is who defines the greater good?

Sources to the map:
Kidron, Michael and Dan Smith, *The New State of War and Peace*, New York: Simon & Schuster, London: HarperCollins, 1991; *Ecumenical Press Service*, Geneva: World Council of Churches.

26 NEVER AGAIN?

Soon after coming to power in 1933, Hitler brought in severe restrictions on the Jewish communities of Germany. In 1940, the systematic rounding up of Jews began, and mass death camps established.

The Holocaust of the Jews under the Nazis was but the latest in a long history of pogroms and other acts of violence against the Jewish race, stretching back over four thousand years. But it was the most cold-blooded and systematic attack on Judaism, resulting in the death of six million Jews. At the same time, some ten million Ukrainian, Russian and Polish soldiers and civilians were imprisoned, of which many millions died in the camps; and over half a million Gypsies and hundreds of thousands of other groups of people such as the physically handicapped, Communists and homosexuals were also murdered in the camps.

The impact of the Nazi persecution on world Judaism goes well beyond the simple fact of so many deaths. It totally altered the geography of Judaism. First of all it virtually wiped out the cultural and historical centres of Judaism in Eastern Europe – in Poland, Lithuania and the Ukraine, and the centres of liberal even secular Judaism, such as Austria and Germany. Secondly, those who could escape went if possible to the USA, thus reinforcing the position of the USA as the country with the world's largest Jewish population – now larger than the state of Israel. Thirdly, it contributed to the creation of the state of Israel, which came into being in 1948.

In the early 1990s, attacks on the Jews continue, as does harassment of other minority groups differentiated by their way of life and beliefs. With the collapse of Communism, anti-semitism as well as general anti-immigrant and anti-Gypsy sentiments have once again been heard. Openly racist or fascist groups exist in a number of countries in Europe and attacks on people and properties belonging to ethnic or religious minorities are increasing. The question in this map's title should be a statement. Never again.

Sources to the map:
Friesel, Evyatar, *Atlas of Modern Jewish History*, Oxford: Oxford University Press, 1990; de Lange, Nicholas, *Atlas of the Jewish World*, London: Guild Publishing, 1984.

Acknowledgements:
Community Research Unit, Board of Deputies of British Jews; Institute of Jewish Affairs, London.

27 FAITH TO FAITH

The interfaith movement is not yet a major movement worldwide. At its most active, it is concentrated in countries with a high level of inter-religious dispute, such as India, the USA or South Africa, or in those where religious tolerance has at least in theory been a hallmark of the state, such as Australia or Germany. Nevertheless, the growth of interfaith work is accelerating, even if it seems to do so in fits and starts and at times lacks direction.

To many people it seems only sensible that people of religious faith – even though the faiths are different – should be able to work together. But the track record of wars and tension in the name of religion bears witness to the intensity of misunderstanding and hatred (see **25. Religion at War**). It was with this in mind that in 1893 the first significant interfaith meeting of the present era took place. At the Chicago International Exhibition of 1893, there was held a World's Parliament of Religions, to which representatives of all the major faiths came. The excitement generated by this meeting was enormous. It seemed like an idea whose time had come.

Throughout the early years of this century, interest in interfaith work increased, as did the number of bodies seeking to promote it. Some were working for a united faith, a new religious unity for humanity. Others tried to overcome the aggression and misunderstanding generated by centuries of opposition or ignorance.

The First World War dealt a severe blow to many people's hopes of a united humanity growing in wisdom. After the war, the interfaith movement slowed down. The experience of the Jewish Holocaust later shook many people within the religious communities. That Christian countries could commit such terrible actions raised the issue of anti-semitism in the Churches. The result was the rise of many Councils of Christians and Jews – pioneer organizations which have made real differences in the ways these two communities relate.

In the 1960s and 1970s, interest and contact increased between religious groups due to expanding opportunities for travel and the growth of sizeable religious minority communities in Europe, North and South America and Australasia, so interest in interfaith contact and dialogue also increased. While not always able to tackle the more turbulent religious issues, the interfaith movement has nevertheless enabled more amicable relations. In many countries it has led to more sympathetic teaching in schools about other faiths.

In some countries, a new interfaith movement has been able to help deal with social, economic or political crises. In the USA, for example, the interfaith movement only really became significant when it emerged out of the crisis of the civil rights movement, and particularly in the aftermath of the assassination of Martin Luther King in 1968. At that time, Jewish, Christian and Muslim leaders sat down to talk and save their neighbourhoods. In

Liberia, where in June 1993, civil war is still raging, the interfaith movement was formed in 1992 to enable Christian and Muslim groups to work together. In 1993, Faith Asylum Refuge (FAR) – an interfaith agency dealing with issues of refugees and migration was set up in the UK alongside other, older, social-issue orientated interfaith groups. And in former Yugoslavia, during 1992 and 1993, Muslim, Christian (both Orthodox and Roman Catholic) and Jewish groups collaborated together in an interfaith network to bring relief to those suffering in the civil war, regardless of creed.

In such contexts, the agenda of interfaith movements is established by the wider society. The faiths work together as best they can, with a common goal of reconciliation and social relief.

The environmental crisis has led to many faiths working collaboratively with each other and with environmental organizations, since no single faith can alone help to solve the fundamental issues which lie behind the abuse of nature (see **30. Down to Earth**).

In certain countries, including Chile and Algeria, the interfaith movement has been initiated by minor faith communities, such as Jews in Argentina and Christians in Algeria. These are often attempts by smaller faiths to have a voice and a more visible presence in order to be seen and heard in overwhelmingly Catholic or Islamic countries.

As part of the 1993 centenary celebrations the Parliament of the World's Religions once again convened in Chicago, as a reminder of the original vision.

Source to the map:
Clark, F., *Interfaith Directory*, New York: International Religious Foundation, 1987.

Acknowledgements:
Wesley Ariarajah; Sub-unit on Dialogue, World Council of Churches, Geneva.

28 THE ECUMENICAL MOVEMENT

The roots of the present worldwide ecumenical movement lie in the missionary experiences of the 19th century. The first major ecumenical, missionary meeting was held in 1910 in Edinburgh, Scotland. In the great vision of that meeting, all Christian Churches would be reunited in one fellowship.

Ecumenical activities were disrupted by the two wars but had gathered strength throughout the inter-war period. When the first assembly of the World Council of Churches (WCC) took place in 1948, it seemed to many as if the movement for reunion between the different branches of Christianity – especially in the Protestant world – was both at hand and inevitable.

Following the Second World War, the Church of North India was created, bringing together Anglicans, Methodists, Presbyterians and Congregationalists into one body; the United Church of Canada combined Methodists, Presbyterians and Congregationalists and a similar reunion led to the Uniting Church of Australia. However, schemes to reunite other denominations, such as the Church of England and the Methodists in the UK, failed despite a number of attempts.

The majority of significant ecumenical schemes for reunion have taken place, as the map shows, in countries where Christianity is a minority faith (as in Sri Lanka, Pakistan and Indonesia) or where both churches and state are fairly new, created during the colonial period (as in Angola, Namibia and New Zealand).

The old, historic dividing grounds of Western Europe (see **32. Foundations**) have at least become places of practical working together between old enemies. Meanwhile parts of Eastern Europe, already split between Roman Catholic, Orthodox and Uniate (Orthodox who belong to Rome) are now experiencing further divisions within these churches as well as the rise of many new Protestant churches. Ironically, by forcing the churches into Councils designed to make state control easier, atheist states such as the former USSR and North Korea have helped some of the churches to work together.

New divisions and tensions have also emerged. In Nigeria, perhaps the most significant example, some five new Christian denominations or splinter churches come into existence every week. The rise of more fundamentalist churches has also led to fragmentation, especially in areas where the Roman Catholic Church has traditionally been strongest, such as Central and northern Latin America. At the end of the 20th century, there are more Christian denominations than at the start of the century and increasing numbers of Christians are practising their faith outside the old denominations and groups.

The World Council of Churches (WCC), the main Protestant and Orthodox world body, with a membership of 400 separate denominations, is committed to unity and better relationships between the churches. Yet these 400 represent only 2 percent of the total worldwide, and only 27 percent of all Christians are in churches officially linked to them. There are ecumenical agendas within the more evangelical churches but these take a secondary place to the drive for mission.

While the Catholic Church is not a member of the World Council of Churches, it is a member of as many as 50 percent of the National Councils of Churches, along with other churches who are not members of the WCC. A much greater number of denominations is therefore involved at local or national levels.

The Councils of Churches have created ecumenical aid agencies; helped to break down barriers of mistrust; set up ecumenical laity training and clergy training and created an atmosphere in which Christians of many different backgrounds can work together. This is especially so in Latin America and African countries, where the issue of reunion is of less importance than liberation, the struggle for justice, or the fight against racism.

The role of the Orthodox Churches in ecumenism has been to work towards reunion with the monophysite Orthodox Churches of Syria, Armenia and Egypt, which split off from the bulk of Orthodoxy in 451. This is a milestone in the reunion of the churches. The Orthodox Churches have been very involved with Councils of Churches and the WCC, but they have not seriously considered unity with Roman Catholic or Protestant groups. Indeed, after the collapse of Communism, they themselves are splitting, as in Bulgaria and the Ukraine.

In the early 1990s, the primary activity of the ecumenical movement is to help the Churches to work together on common concerns rather than try to achieve a United Church.

Source for the map:
Ecumenical Press Service, Geneva: World Council of Churches.

Acknowledgements:
Martin Reardon; Churches Together In England, London.

29 EQUAL RITES

According to most criteria, all the major world religions are essentially patriarchal in their power structures, deities and formats. Within some religions there are still significant manifestations of the divine feminine (see **12. Faith in the Feminine**), but they are usually subservient – at least in official teaching – to male figures and authorities.

It may be difficult to question why it is almost exclusively men, such as the Buddha, Krishna, Jesus, Muhammad and so forth, who are the key figures in their respective faiths, but the women's movement has gone some way to focus attention on the male-dominated structures of the major religions. In the case of Christianity, this has focused upon the role of women at a sacramental and pastoral level – the role of priests and ministers. In Buddhism it has focused upon the right of women to belong to a religious order – to be members of the Sangha alongside monks. In Judaism, it is not only the role of the rabbi which has come under scrutiny but the participation of women generally in public religious life.

In theory, at least, the majority of mainstream Protestant denominations within Christianity offer complete equality to women at almost all levels of the church. All the major Protestant denominations now ordain women – although this is in debate or not yet begun in a few areas or denominations. In the Episcopal Church of the USA, the Anglican Church in New Zealand, the Methodist Church of the USA and the Lutheran churches, there are now women bishops. However, resistance is still strong and the churches may be more resistant to change than society at large.

The debate has been particularly fierce within the Church of England and its worldwide body, the Anglican Communion (including, amongst others, Episcopalians in the USA and the Anglican Church of New Zealand). While the threats of a major split have failed to materialize in all instances, the decision to ordain women has created very heated debate and may lead to small numbers leaving the church to form traditionalist churches. The pie-chart on the Anglican Communion illustrates the growth of women's ordained ministry in the churches – over 50 percent of all Anglican Communion churches now ordain women and in

1993 there are three women bishops.

The Roman Catholic Church has as yet to make any significant move on the position of women in the church and will make none under Pope John Paul II. However, groups are now being formed in a number of countries, such as Ireland, the USA and Germany to press for the ordination of women. Many theologians are in favour and have openly voiced their support. During Communist persecution of the Roman Catholic Church in former Czechoslovakia, a woman was ordained at least to deacon level, if not to full priesthood. She has now decided to remain silent, but the precedent stands. In similar circumstances, the first Anglican woman priest was ordained in China in 1944.

Due to the decline in the number of priests (see **15. A Worldwide Church**), women in many parts of the world are already playing a much greater role in parishes and in specialized ministries such as hospitals and prisons. In the Base Christian Communities, radical lay-orientated communities in the impoverished areas of South America, women play a major role. The experience, combined with the need for more priests, the rise of gender issues generally and the Czechoslovakia precedent, means that the Roman Catholic Church will probably decide in favour of women priests in the not-far-distant future.

In Russian Orthodox churches, a ceremony already exists for ordaining women as deacons – the final rung before ordination to the priesthood. Yet this has lain unused for centuries and Orthodox Church opinion is that it is an issue for the future.

The key dates on the role of women within the Protestant churches show that some churches have been ahead of society in their attitude to women's equality. The Quakers were part of that upsurge of radical thinking in the wake of the English Civil War of the 1640s. The Salvation Army gave full equality from its foundation in 1869, long before women were granted the right to vote in most countries.

In Buddhism, often under pressure from Western Buddhists, the issue of equal rights of participation at all levels by women has led to a revival of interest in women's orders. In some Buddhist countries (notably Tibet and Thailand) the order of nuns died out long ago. The question now revolves around whether any women's orders from places such as China – which has always maintained one – can restore the tradition to other countries. It is a question of continuing authority, but it has also challenged the strong patriarchal assumptions of many traditional Buddhist countries. In Thailand it is seen as being part of the whole debate about the role of women in Thai society and about the extent to which Western values can be merged with traditional Buddhist values.

In Judaism, only the Reform and Liberal wings ordain women as rabbis. Orthodox Jews are opposed. In common with many Christian women, Jewish women scholars are now engaged in extensive re-examination of the Biblical records to show how patriarchy suppressed a more equal relationship between men and women.

One aspect of this research has led to a significant debate in both Judaism and Christianity. This is the issue of whether God can be addressed as both Father (He) and Mother (She). This questioning of the assumptions of language about the nature of God has sent considerable shock waves through more traditional sections of the faiths, but has also opened up a major debate and exploration of basic notions of the Godhead.

Islam does not have the same sort of debate. For many in Islam, the women's movement as a whole is just another sign of the faltering society of the West. Islam's response has often been to claim that Islam is the true liberator of women. Muslims have questioned what liberation entails and refer to the harrassment that women suffer as a result of ambiguous sexual roles. Many Muslims point to the increase in sexual violence and to the stresses and demands made on women, and ask what sort of liberation this is. Islam sees these as signs of a disruption of a natural order ordained by God. Yet under Islamic law women have had the right to own land and property in their own right since the time of Muhammad, whereas women in the West only achieved such rights this century. However, in traditional Muslim countries, as in the West, women have been asking for greater freedom and opportunity for equal participation in society. In countries where militant Islam has recently gained strength, changes in women's clothing and behaviour away from the traditional Islamic model have been condemned and prohibited.

Acknowledgements:
Caroline Davis; Jenny Standage; Anglican Consultative Council, London; Ecumenical Press Service, World Council of Churches, Geneva; Lutheran World Federation Women's Desk, Geneva; Methodist Overseas Division, London; Movement for the Ordination of Women, London.

30 DOWN TO EARTH

In 1967 an American environmentalist, Lynn White, published a watershed article claiming that the roots of the contemporary environmental crisis lay in Judeo-Christian culture. The command in the Book of Genesis, the first book of the Bible, that humanity should have dominion over all other species, he saw as the root of our use and abuse of nature. White raised a storm of debate about the relationship between religion and the environment which continues to this day.

In 1986, the World Wide Fund for Nature International invited five major religions to Assisi, Italy, birthplace of St Francis, the Roman Catholic saint of ecology, to discuss and plan for greater religious involvement in the environmental movement. Eight religions now belong to the Network on Conservation and Religion established at Assisi: Baha'is, Buddhists, Christians, Hindus, Jains, Jews, Muslims and Sikhs.

The impetus of the Assisi meeting, plus a rise of general awareness within the faiths, means that there are now hundreds, if not thousands, of religious-directed environmental projects around the world: through the work of religious aid agencies (from the mid- to late 1980s); through education; through practical projects such as tree planting in India or Thailand, or species conservation in English churchyards.

Our map does not attempt to measure levels of environmental awareness but shows where religions have responded to environmental issues and which religions have done so. In only some states are the religions shown to be involved in environmental problems abroad as well as at home. This may be due more to differences in economic well-being than in levels of commitment.

Although the problems of the environment were first highlighted by secular environmental groups, religious involvement in the environment is undertaken from religious principles and beliefs, and not just in response to secular agendas. They may at first have been seen as 'soft' issues, but the religions are realizing that the well-being of the environment is closely connected to fundamental economic and social issues. The environmental crisis has caused a major rethinking within all faiths. The faiths are showing that they can work side by side on the environment, in a way that is unique in history – even in areas of traditional hostility such as the Lebanon and the Philippines.

In a number of wealthy countries, the religious aid agencies are now adding an environmental focus to their projects and emphasizing the link between the environment and development. This link was strongly enforced at the UNCED Earth Summit in Rio de Janeiro, in 1992.

Acknowledgements:
Joni Seager; Education Unit, World Wide Fund for Nature, UK; Network on Conservation and Religion, WWF International, Geneva.

31 FAITH IN THE FUTURE

Looking into the future, even for an atlas on religion, is a risky business. But as everyone, including big business and the military, engages in the 'art and science of futurism', so do we!

We expect the gradual spread of secularism to continue, reaching into most aspects of life, in countries as diverse as Ireland, Japan and Malaysia. In many parts of Western Europe, in Australasia and Canada, the growth of secularism will be largely at the cost of institutional Christianity as expressed in the major denominations. It will also affect minority faith communities, such as Jews, Muslims and Hindus, as constraints on the young of family ties weaken.

Although a growth of religion has been set in motion by the collapse of Communism, well-established secularism will simply continue in some states of the former USSR and Eastern Europe. In 10 to 15 years' time it may even increase as memory of the Communist system fades or its reputation is revived. In Poland, in particular, we expect an increase in secularism, in reaction to the powerful hold of the Roman Catholic Church and tensions between state and church which are already evident.

In Malaysia, a majority Muslim country, secularism will spread as a result of wider educational opportunities and the attractions of Western consumerism. The same trend can be discerned in Buddhist Japan and the Christian Philippines.

In the very areas where secularism is growing, we expect a rise in religious diversity. Interest in things spiritual, in Western Europe, Australasia and Japan, for example, is no longer confined to the historic majority faiths of these countries. With the collapse of belief in many previous religious authority structures, interest in exploring other religious models will grow. In all such states there will be some growth in New Religious Movements. More significant will be the growth of interest in major faiths other than the existing majority faith: in Western Europe and North America, in Buddhism, Hinduism and Taoism; in Malaysia, Buddhism and possibly Christianity.

We believe there will be a greater willingness to belong to small, intimate and non-hierarchical religious groups and a tendency to reject the more structured and authoritarian. This is already happening in many Christian countries, such as the USA, the UK and France. This tendency gives the traditional faiths an opportunity to re-express themselves, with the promise of regained strength.

The collapse of Communism in the USSR and Eastern Europe may be followed by changes in Cuba, North Korea and even China. For Christianity the picture is very varied. In eastern Germany there has been little increase in the number of active Christians. In Poland, Russia and Bulgaria however, the new freedoms have led to a massive revival of the churches. This revival, and the excitement it generates, could well spill over into the more jaded Western Europe. There is also a risk, certainly understood by leaders of the Russian Orthodox Church, that raised and often unrealistic expectations are being placed upon the churches by often desperate people. This may lead to disillusionment and tension.

In the emerging states of Central Asia, the fall of Communism has led to the rise of Islam. Some are looking for an Iranian-style strict Islamic state based on Shari'ah. Others are looking for a more Turkish, secular model, in which religion nevertheless has an honoured place. The outcome will be significant. Iranian-style states will increase religious tension and a missionary drive in bordering states such as Turkey, China and Russia. Turkish-style states will influence trade and commerce more than Islam.

Buddhism will continue to recover in China and other Communist or nationalist areas of Asia, and continue to spread to the West. It may be affected and changed, however, by the same factors facing Christianity and Islam in their recovery from Communism. Such changes could even be fuelled by the arrival of Western Buddhism in Asia.

A further growth area for religion is what is termed fundamentalism or conservatism – a quest for assurance and certainty with regard to basic religious values and truths. This appeal for a moral, ethical and religious code which allows for little or no accommodation to anti- or non-religious standards is highly attractive to those confused and disturbed by social, political and religious change. While this return to fundamentals may be interpreted as a backwards movement, it also has revolutionary potential. This is visible in the appeal of the Islamic movements of Central Asia, the nationalist Orthodox politics of right-wing groups in Russia, and in the popularity of extreme nationalist Hinduism in India.

Fundamentalism posits perhaps the only serious challenge to the growth of rational, consumerist, secular society. Now that Communism has gone, fundamentalism is being seen by some scholars as the new opposition. In some states, it is already on the rise against Western society. Militant Muslims in Egypt and extremist Christians in South Africa represent the more disturbing and backward-looking aspects of this trend. Given the appeal of fundamentalism to most of the poor world (whether whole states as in Central Asia or poor communities such as the urban poor of Central America and the black urban poor of the USA), those preaching fundamentalism within the different religions have begun to take social and political issues seriously. The potential for the rise in fundamentalism to become a major voice of the oppressed could radically alter not just religious but political maps around the world.

Serious religious tensions, bringing war and civil war, continue to increase (see **25. Religion at War**): in Nigeria, between Muslims and Christians; in the whole of the Balkans involving Muslims and Christians; in India between Muslims and Hindus, Sikhs and Hindus; in Malaysia between indigenous peoples and the state; in Egypt, between militant Islam and the state.

The historic Christian communities of Western Asia (the Near and Middle East) will continue to emigrate as Islamic militancy grows. Highly localized expressions of ancient Christianity are now scattered over fifty to seventy different countries worldwide. Also the result of migration, the rise of small but significant Islamic communities in Europe means greater religious diversity and may lead either to greater tensions or to a more equitable relationship between Muslims and the host communities.

Christianity and Islam will continue to spread across the world, especially in Asia and Africa and largely at the expense of traditional belief. Burkina Faso is likely to become a majority Muslim country and Togo will become a majority Christian country. However, the encounter will produce more hybrid groups which fuse elements of Christianity or Islam with traditional belief.

Traditional belief may also lose ground in China. With the gradual removal of more strict Marxist-Leninist-Mao Tse Tung thought, the Chinese are not only turning back to traditional ways but also towards Christianity and a revitalized Chinese Buddhism.

All the major religions are now accessible across most of the world. As yet, most people still follow the main historic religion of their area. However, the rise of Christianity and Islam is continuing so rapidly that pluralism may in some states replace the traditional notion of a majority religion. South Korea, for example, is shifting away from its historic faith (in this case Buddhism) and into being a majority Christian state.

The indigenous Christian churches of Africa, radical forms of Judaism in the USA, new versions of Buddhism in the West – all these are arising in places far removed from their historic centres. Religion only survives when it is able to change. The rapidity of change at present, and the widespread and diverse nature of many faiths, make it difficult to say what will eventually emerge.

Source to the map:
Barrett, David B., *Cosmos, Chaos and Gospel*, Birmingham, Alabama: New Hope, 1987.

32 FOUNDATIONS

The historic roots of the world's major religions and their divisions lie in a swathe across the 'old' world: from Europe, across the Middle East, India and up into China and Japan. These are the roots of Buddhism in Nepal, north India, Tibet, South-East Asia, China and Japan; of Christianity in Europe and Western Asia; of Hinduism in India; Islam in Western Asia and North Africa; and Judaism in the Middle East and Eastern Europe. Over the centuries these have been the centres of the great faiths as well as the source of their most significant divisions, all of which still exist today.

Over the last 50 years in particular, many new and varied expressions of all the major faiths have come into being (see **10. New Religious Movements**) but so far none has captured significant worldwide support. The vast majority of those who claim allegiance to one of the major world religions would still identify themselves with the sub-divisions shown on our map.

Both Shi'a and Sunni Muslims see themselves as being more faithful to the original Islam declared by the prophet Muhammad. Yet in Islamic history, it is customary to see the move of the capital, from Medina to Kufa in 657 by the Caliph Ali to escape the control of those opposed to him, as being the turning point which led to the distinct identity of the Shi'ites. As no such turning point is usually given for Sunni Muslims, we have not recorded them on the map.

Within Christianity, the division between the Orthodox Churches and the Catholic Church is variously dated to 1054, the 8th century CE and even to 451 CE. We therefore show the Orthodox Church as having arisen from the first conversions of Greeks to the Gospel in Jerusalem in 33 CE, and the foundation of the Church in Rome to 50 CE. Dates for the foundation of certain Protestant groups accord with the first emergence of their distinct identity, in a form which has continued to today. The church in England for example, dates from c.70 CE. However, Anglicanism as something separate from the Roman Catholic Church dates from 1536, when the king replaced the Pope as head of the church.

Sources to the map:
Cross, F.L., ed., *Oxford Dictionary of the Christian Church*, Oxford: Oxford University Press, 1957; Hinnells, John, R., *Who's Who of World Religions*, London: Macmillan, 1991; de Lange, Nicholas, *Atlas of the Jewish World*, London: Guild Publishing, 1984; Snelling, John, *The Buddhist Handbook*, London: Rider, 1987.

Acknowledgements:
Elizabeth Breuilly; Mawil Izzidien.

33 HOLY CITIES

Nearly all the major religions have arisen from predominantly agricultural or small town cultures. For the faithful, the city can symbolize danger and opportunity. When a new city is created on religious principles, great hopes are placed upon it. Yet no ideal city has ever been created and cities, by their very nature, are 'impure', cosmopolitan places, full of challenging ideas and cultures.

Makkah in Saudi Arabia represents the desire for a religious city; no non-Muslim is allowed to enter Makkah and strict religious laws are enforced. Other significant ones are Salt Lake City in the USA, which was built in the 19th century as a refuge for persecuted Mormons; and Amritsar in India, built and developed in the 16th and 17th centuries, as a centre for the oppressed Sikhs.

However, most holy cities have become holy not because they were built as such, but because of events or persons associated with them. Jerusalem is holy to three faiths: to Jews because it holds the site of the Temple, the original focus of Jewish religious life, which some believe must be rebuilt if the promised Messiah is to come and end all suffering; to Christians because of Jesus, his crucifixion and resurrection; and to Muslims because of Muhammad's night journey from the Dome of the Rock, on the site of the Jewish Temple, to Heaven. In all three faiths, there is also an interesting division between the Jerusalem which is an ordinary city, complete with ordinary human failings, and the Jerusalem idealized as a holy city in both mythology and theology.

Many great holy towns and cities combine places of transcendent beauty, in an atmosphere of holiness, with the squalor of commerce, exploitation, poor food and accommodation, cheap trinkets and souvenirs, plus other 'services' for the traveller away from home. The tawdry side of holy places and those who gather for profit around them can often cause offence to both believers and non-believers alike.

In the Middle Ages, Europeans travelled widely throughout Europe and the Middle East to visit holy towns and sites. They enjoyed their pursuit of holiness, and came for many different reasons – as Chaucer's *The Canterbury Tales* makes clear. With the advent of the Protestant Reformation, pilgrimages and holy sites were considered popish and pagan and were banned in Protestant areas, especially in England. Within a few generations, secular pilgrimage routes were developed – the foundations of modern tourism. These routes still often went to holy cities – Rome and Athens or Constantinople – but did so in a spirit of adventure rather than devotion. Today, especially in smaller but popular cities such as Assisi in Italy or Katmandu in Nepal, tourist invasions by people not sharing the devotion of the faithful can create tensions with those who come to worship.

Some holy cities become a focal point of power struggles between faiths or between ethnic/religious groups. In Jerusalem, the most striking example, after centuries of conflict there is still tension between Jews, Muslims and Christians. In India in 1985, Amritsar was stormed by Indian government troops to break the power of a group calling for Sikh independence. In 1992 in Ayodhya, also in India, a mosque built on the reputed site of the Hindu god Rama's birthplace was destroyed – signalling a further outbreak of militant Hinduism. Lhasa, in Tibet, is a holy city largely destroyed during the last 50 years; China has set out to break Tibetan religious identity and brought in so many Han Chinese that they may now represent as much as 60 percent of the city's population.

Sources to the map:
Crowther, G., P.A. Raj and T. Wheeler, *India: A Travel Survival Kit*, South Yarra, Australia: Lonely Planet, 1981; Harvey, Peter, *An Introduction to Buddhism*, Cambridge, Cambridge University Press, 1990; Hinnells, John, ed., *Penguin Dictionary of Religions*, Harmondsworth: Penguin, 1984; Russell, Jeremy, *The Eight Places of Buddhist Pilgrimage*, New Delhi: Mahayana Publications, 1981; Walker, B., *Hindu World*, London: George Allen and Unwin, 1968.

Acknowledgements:
Iftikhar Awan; Rupert Gethin; Mawil Izzidien; Ranchor Prime; Aubrey Rose.

34 HOLY NATURAL

In many cultures, natural beauty has been celebrated as being in some special sense divine. Hinduism, Taoism and traditional beliefs, for instance, consider all of nature to be in some way sacred. Certain sites are especially revered. Specific deities or stories may come to be associated with them, but usually their holiness stems from their sheer awe-inspiring presence. In this map we have focused only on those sites of significance within the major world religions. It would have been impossible on the scale available to include the vast number of sites associated with traditional beliefs, although Australian aborigines and the Kikuyu of Kenya, to name just two examples, have many sacred natural sites.

Mountains are the most common natural feature to be revered as holy. Often rising dramatically from the plains, as do Mount Ararat and Mount Sinai, it is easy to see why they have been special places since ancient times. Remoteness and the hardship experienced by those who try to live on them are also a part of their appeal. This is especially true of the major holy mountains of China. Chinese poets, painters and mystics have always found mountains to have particular significance. The Chinese character for a sage or immortal combines the characters for a person and a mountain.

The Celts, both Christian and pre-Christian, found water and islands especially mystical and islands still exert special attraction for the religious mind, offering solitude and peace. They may also feature a mountain (the interaction of water and mountain has extra power) be difficult to reach, and be cut off from the easier ways of the mainland. Most holy islands are small and may become closely associated with a particular religious figure: on Patmos in the Aegean, of John the Divine; on Iona, off the coast of Scotland, of Columba; on Pu-to island, off the coast of China, of the Buddhist goddess Kuan Yin. Unlike other holy islands, the island of Shikoku is very large, yet it is wholly associated with a key religious figure, Kobo Daishi, who made a one thousand mile pilgrimage route around the island.

The flowing of rivers and the cycle of rainfall, river and evaporation may be readily linked with the cycle of life. In the Ganges, the most revered river in India, this connection is closest, since it is through the river, according to Hindu belief, that souls return to their origin and are later reborn. The use of water for washing may be associated with the act of washing away sins and evil – as, for example, the River Jordan in Israel.

Belief in sacred natural places helps to preserve our natural environment as a whole. Farming and killing are not usually allowed around holy places and, in these areas, wildlife and their habitat is especially protected. As the major faiths recognize the importance of the environment, holy natural sites are taking on a new significance. Some faiths are now looking to take the notion of sacred land out to a wider audience.

Sources for the map:

Jackson, B., *Places of Pilgrimage*, London: Geoffrey Chapman, 1989; Naquin, S. and Chun-sang Yu, eds., *Pilgrimage and Sacred Sites in China*, Berkeley, California: University of California Press, 1992; Richards, H.J., *Pilgrimage to the Holy Land*, Great Wakering, Essex: Mayhew McCrimmon, 1985.

Other Pluto Projects Available from Touchstone Books!

THE NEW STATE OF WAR AND PEACE

Edited by Michael Kidron and Dan Smith

Concise and up-to-the-minute, with 37 full-color international maps, this completely new and indispensable military atlas provides an easy-to-understand survey of the arsenals, armies, and alliances around the globe.

0-671-70103-7, paper, $14.95

THE NEW STATE OF THE WORLD ATLAS

Michael Kidron and Ronald Segal

Combining 50 all-new colorful maps, graphs, and text, this updated 4th edition encapsulates the real state of finances, governments, societies, and the environment in our rapidly changing world.

0-671-74556-5, paper, $15.00

"Unique and uniquely beautiful. . . .A single map here tells us more about the world today than a dozen statistical abstracts or scholarly tomes."

— *Los Angeles Times*

Simon & Schuster/Touchstone
1230 Avenue of the Americas, New York, NY 10020